AN INDUCTIVE BIBLE STUDY ON THE BOOK OF JOHN

just Jesus

Journey with John as He Points You to Jesus

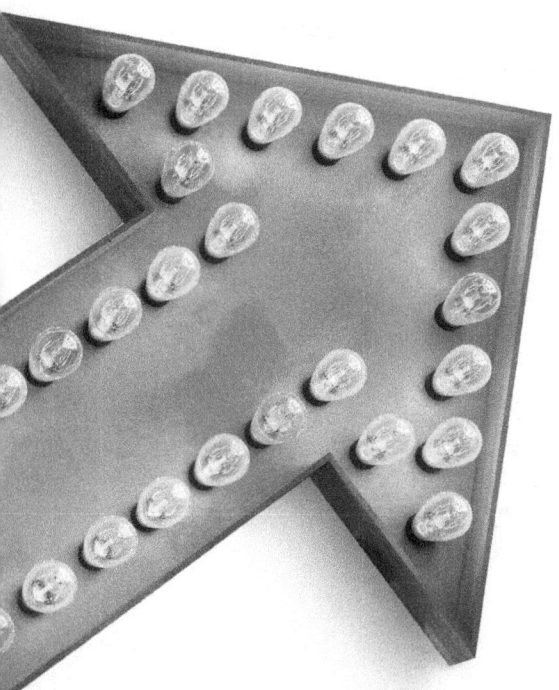

SHELLY FROST

Bright-Eyed Urchin Publishing

Just Jesus

Journey with John as He Points You to Jesus

Published by Bright-Eyed Urchin Publishing. ©2018 by Shelly Frost
All Rights Reserved. No part of this bible study may be reproduced or transmitted in any form without prior written permission of the publisher.

Original Printing, 2018
ISBN 978-0-9996534-0-1

Unless otherwise stated,
Scripture quotations are taken from the HOLY BIBLE, NEW INTERNATIONAL VERSION, Copyright © 1973, 1978, 1984 by International Bible Society. Used by permission of Zondervan Publishing House. All rights reserved.
Scripture quotations marked "The Message" are taken from THE MESSAGE. Copyright © 1993, 1994, 1995, 1996, 2000, 2001, 2002. Used by permission of NavPress Publishing Group.
Scripture quotations marked "NLT" are taken from The Holy Bible, New Living Translation, copyright © 1996, 2004. Used by permission of Tyndale House Publishers, Inc., Wheaton, Illinois 60189. All rights reserved.

Editing by Shelly Frost at Bright-Eyed Urchin Publishing
Layout by Melinda Martin at Martin Publishing Services and Jonathan Lewis at Jonlin Creative
Cover design by Melinda Martin at Martin Publishing Services

Dedication and Thanks

This bible study is dedicated to my kids, Matt and Taylor. Aside from the bible, you have taught me more than anything in this world. You will find God in the pages of His Word. I hope I have (at least the majority of the time) demonstrated that He is worth finding. I love you both so much, and He loves you more.

Thank you . . .

Jeff – I could not have done this without you allowing me to stay home to do it. Thank you for working so hard so I could work on this. I love you.

Mom – You have always been my biggest cheerleader. Thank you for your encouragement and your words of affirmation on the long road here.

Karen – I will forever be grateful for the opportunity and the challenge you presented me. Thank you for believing in me.

My small group guinea pigs – thank you for trusting me to lead you to the feet of Jesus and for your gentle and gracious feedback.

Father,

You are trustworthy. You have been faithful in my life and I believe You will be faithful here, once again. Thank you for everything you taught me through this journey, about John, about myself, and mostly about Jesus. I love Him more. Reveal Him to every person who does this study. Show them Jesus and let them fall madly in love with Him. You promised me over and over again as I wrote that You would teach the people who did this study. You said it was my job to get them into Your Word and that You would teach each one of them exactly what You wanted them to learn while they studied it. I believe I've done my part, Lord. Now it's all on You. The vision of that big, lighted arrow sign is as clear today as it was the first time You gave it to me. May this study be that arrow pointing others to Your Son. And may You receive all the glory.

Preface

This bible study has been an act of love, which is fitting considering the Book of John is all about love. It has been an act of love on my part because my love for God displayed itself in obedience: risking failing for Him. It was an act of love from God, because He decided to show up once again when I asked Him to, and He'll do the same for you.

I don't pretend to be an expert on the bible or bible study. It kills the teacher and recovering perfectionist in me to say that I am absolutely certain I have gotten some things wrong in here. I am not a trained Theologian. What I am is a fellow student of God's Word who wants desperately for you to know Him or to know Him better.

I don't claim to have any super powers of bible study other than the One God has planted in me that helped me write this study and Who helps me understand God's Word every time I open it. To write this study I prayed and asked God to reveal to me what He wanted whoever would do this study to focus on. Then I listened and paid attention to His still soft voice every time it made me aware of something He wanted to camp on. I am confident He heard my prayers because I would have chosen to focus on different segments than He wanted us to.

There were times when I tried to convince Him He was skipping over really important parts of scripture, because I hadn't heard Him tell us to camp there, but He wouldn't budge. This study is not an exhaustive, all-you-ever-need-to-know-from-the-book-of-John study. It's the study I believe God wants you to do on the book of John during this season of your life. He's going to make it personal, if you let Him. His Word is alive and active and sharper than any double-edged sword. And only He knows where that sword needs to be pointed in your life, today. I don't know what God wants to teach you through this study, but I know He will teach you, if you will listen. He can't wait to teach you, in fact. I am confident He will be faithful to do His part, and I am praying that you find joy and peace as you do yours.

Whether you have known Jesus all your life or you've just heard His Name for the first time, my prayer is that you get to know Him while you do this study. If He tells you to skip questions, feel free. If He brings questions to your mind while you're studying, by all means write them down and take them up in your small group time. He will speak to you. Practice listening.

Where I have quoted directly I have documented my sources in the back of the study. Biblical quotes are from the New International Version unless otherwise noted. I've also listed materials and websites I used in studying the book of John, in case you are interested. For the most part, www.blueletterbible.org is the online study tool I used, but feel free to use another if you have a favorite.

Table of Contents

Introduction 2
Main Events in the Book of John 3
Introduction to John 5
John Chapter One – Part I 9
John Chapter One – Part II 21
John Chapter Two 29
John Chapter Three 39
John Chapter Four 47
John Chapter Five 57
John Chapter Six 65
John Chapter Seven 77
John Chapter Eight 85
John Chapter Nine 99
John Chapter Ten 107
John Chapter Eleven 113
John Chapter Twelve 123
John Chapter Thirteen 135
John Chapter Fourteen 143
John Chapter Fifteen 155
John Chapter Sixteen 165
John Chapter Seventeen 171
John Chapter Eighteen 183
John Chapter Nineteen 199
John Chapter Twenty 215
John Chapter Twenty-One 225
About This Study 231
    For the Participant 231
    For the Leader 232
    Small Group Covenant 234
    Form letter email for the person sharing his/her testimony 236
Song List for Just Jesus 237
Works Cited 238

Introduction

Dear Fellow Journeyer,

"Just Jesus" - that's all we really need. Plain and simple; just Jesus. The book of John is an eye-witness account of Jesus' life. While it's full of miracles and drama, it is at its roots, a simple love story. And John's purpose is simple too; to introduce people to Jesus.

This study may be a bit different from other studies you've done. Instead of separating the homework into days, I've only separated it into weeks for you. Believing that the Holy Spirit will guide and teach you as you do your homework, I didn't feel I had the right to suggest when you should stop in your studies, and I felt dividing it into days would do that. So, enjoy doing your homework when you want and take a break when you feel led to, but I encourage you to do it the week it's assigned, as John has twenty-one chapters and it would be easy to fall behind.

You may also notice there's not a lot of fluff in this workbook. No drawings or pictures and not a lot of commentary. I enjoy the creative pictures, quotes and commentary authors often add to supplement their works as much as the next girl, but I think sometimes authors feel like they have to add to the bible to make studying it fun. *There is nothing I could add that would make the bible more effective than it is on its own.* My hope is that by simply pointing you to scripture, you won't be distracted by fluff and you will be able to see the simple messages at the heart of it.

I ask you to use an online bible study tool and I suggest you use a Study Bible that has notes and commentary on verses within it. Your understanding of the book of John will be more complete if you do these things, but if you can't, the Holy Spirit will still teach you what He wants you to learn during the time you set apart to hear from Him.

The vision God gave me continuously while writing this study was of a big metal sign, shaped like an arrow with large white bulbs outlining it. It was the kind of sign you'd see in front of a country dance hall or a barbeque restaurant, directing you to come on in and try it. This bible study is that arrow, pointing you to Jesus in scripture. In fact, I feel strongly that this study is of little value other than being that arrow. Its purpose is to help you meet Jesus in the pages of the bible.

Thank you for trusting me enough to follow me in the direction of that arrow,

Shelly

Main Events in the Book of John

1. _____
2. _____
3. _____
4. _____
5. _____
6. _____
7. _____
8. _____
9. _____
10. _____
11. _____
12. _____
13. _____
14. _____
15. _____
16. _____
17. _____
18. _____
19. _____
20. _____
21. _____

***When you've finished, take a minute to look back. Do most of your lines start with the same word, Jesus?**

Introduction to John

INTRODUCTION

Please use the introduction section to the book of John in your study bible, an online bible study tool, and/or a commentary on the book of John to answer the following questions:

1. Who wrote the book of John? Write down some facts about his family and life.

   _____

   _____

   _____

   _____

Go to www.blueletterbible.org online

- Type "John 1" in the Search the Bible verse, word or topic box
- Click on "tools" to the left of John 1:1
- Click on the "commentaries" tab to choose a commentary on the book of John

*You can use this tool for any verse you want. Just enter your verse in the Search the Bible verse, word or topic box.

2. To whom was the book written? _____

   _____

   _____

3. When was the book written? _____

   _____

   _____

4. What was happening historically when the stories in the book took place?

   _____

   _____

   _____

   _____

JUST JESUS

Check out the New Testament time line at www.blueletterbible.org

- Type "John" in the Search the Bible verse, word or topic box
- Click on "tools" to the left of John 1:1
- Click on the "misc" tab to look at maps, timelines and other images related to John 1:1

Google "Key Places in the Book of John" to view maps of where the stories in John took place.

5. Take a look at a New Testament timeline, noting when the events in the book of John took place. God had been silent for four hundred years. During that time, which is often called the Intertestamental Period, Israel had heard nothing from God. Everything changed when He sent His Word, Jesus.

6. When did the events in John take place? _____

7. Where was the book written? _____

8. Spend some time online familiarizing yourself with some bible time maps of the land surrounding the Mediterranean and Aegean Seas. Notice where Ephesus, Rome, the Island of Patmos and the area where Jesus traveled are.

9. Since the book of John is about Jesus' life, use a map noting the Key Places in John and the points below to trace Jesus' travels from the beginning of His public ministry through His death and resurrection. Keep in mind that John was on many of these journeys with Jesus.

- His ministry began in Bethany, East of the Jordan, where He was baptized by John the Baptist

- He performed His first miracle in Cana at a wedding feast where He turned water into wine.

- He traveled to and then lived in Capernaum.

- He went to Jerusalem to celebrate every feast of the Lord.

- He traveled through Judea, Samaria, and Galilee.

- Near Bethsaida He fed the five thousand.

- He walked on water on the Sea of Galilee

- Then He traveled through Galilee, to Jerusalem, to Perea.

- He raised Lazarus from the dead in Bethany

- He finished His ministry on earth in Jerusalem where He celebrated and forever changed the Passover.

10. Why did John write this book? What was his reason or purpose for writing it?

_____

_____

_____

11. Using your study bible, write a rough outline of the Book of John, giving titles to each of the sections below:

    - Ch 1-11 – _____

    - Ch 12-19 – _____

    - Ch 13-17 – _____

    - Ch 20-21 – _____

It is interesting to note that of the twenty-one chapters in the book of John:

- the first eleven chapters are about Jesus' life and ministry, which lasted approximately thirty-three years.

- the next eight chapters (12-19) focus on events that took place during one week of Jesus' life.

- the final two chapters are about when Jesus came back to life and what He did for those final forty days.

John wanted us to be aware of the miracles Jesus had performed and the life He had lived, so he spent eleven chapters on those thirty-three years, but our author's main goal was for us to know what Jesus did for us on the cross, which is why he spent so much time on that one week of Jesus' life.

> Eight of the twenty-one chapters in the book of John focus on the events that took place during the last week of Jesus' life.

12. Use your online study tool to find the main themes in the book of John.

    _____
    _____
    _____
    _____
    _____
    _____

13. Why do you think John chose to include about 75% new material in his eye-witness of Jesus' life, rather than repeating the same stories offered in the other gospel accounts? _____

    _____
    _____

14. Please read Matthew 4:18-22, to learn the story of how our author, John, became a follower of Jesus.

John Chapter One – Part I

1. Spend some time listening to one of your favorite worship songs to get you focused on Jesus. Pray and ask God to teach you through His word as you study it. Ask Him to reveal hidden secrets and to open your eyes to what He wants you to learn in this time.

2. Please read John 1:1-34.

3. Use an online bible study tool to look up the original meaning of the word translated "beginning" in John 1:1.

4. What is the Strong's Concordance number for that word? _____

5. What is the original word? _____

6. What was its original meaning? _____
   _____
   _____
   _____

7. What does the word, "he" refer to in John 1:2? _____

8. What is John trying to teach us about Jesus in verses 1-2? _____
   _____
   _____

Go to www.blueletterbible.org

- Type "John 1:1" in the Search the Word verse, word or topic box
- Click on "tools" to the left of John 1:1
- Look through the "interlinear" tab to find the word you are looking for, in this case, "beginning". You will find the Strong's number for that word in the column under "Strong's". The original word is to the right of the Strong's number, in the "Root Transliterated" column.
- To learn the original word's meaning, click on the Strong's number.

beginning:

Strong's number – G746

original word – arche

meaning – origin, the person or thing that commences, the first person in a series, the leader, that by which anything begins to be

JUST JESUS

9. The same word is used in Revelation 22:13. What does that verse say?

   _____

   _____

10. Use an online bible study tool to look up the original meaning of the word translated "the Word" in John 1:1. See the text box near question #3 for directions.

11. What is the Strong's Concordance number for that word? _____

12. What is the original word? _____

13. What was its original meaning? _____

   _____

   _____

   _____

the Word:

   Strong's number – G3056

   original word – logos

   meaning – a word, what someone has said, a topic, the Divine Expression

14. Now look at Genesis 1:1. What is the original word translated as, "beginning" here? _____

15. Although this word is in Hebrew, because it's in the Old Testament, its meaning is similar to a word we studied before. What was that word again?

   _____

16. Skim through the rest of Genesis 1. What phrase does each of the paragraphs begin with? _____

17. What, then, did God use to create everything? _____

CHAPTER 1 – PART I

God created everything with His breath, His spoken word. He didn't have to lift a finger.

18. Why is it so important to John for us to understand that the Word, Jesus, has always existed? _____

    _____

    _____

    _____

    _____

19. In John 1:6 we are introduced to another John in scripture. Which John is our author talking about here? _____

20. Please read Luke 1:5-80 to gain a better understanding of who John the Baptist was and how he was related to Jesus. Who were John the Baptist's parents and how was John the Baptist related to Jesus? _____

    _____

    _____

John the Baptist's mom was Elizabeth. Jesus' mom was Mary. Elizabeth and Mary were cousins. John the Baptist was six months older than Jesus.

21. Use your online bible study tools to learn more about John the Baptist and write down three interesting facts you learn. _____

    _____

    _____

    _____

22. If you pay close attention to the first eighteen verses of John 1, the author wavers back and forth between paragraphs about John the Baptist and Jesus. Why do you think he did that? _____

_____

_____

_____

23. In John 1:19 John begins to tell us about the mere man, John the Baptist. When the priests and Levites asked John the Baptizer who he was, how did he respond? _

24. Why do you think John the Baptizer tells us who he isn't instead of who he is?

_____

_____

_____

_____

25. Do you think it's significant that John answers them three times who he is not before he tells them who he is? _____

_____

_____

26. Let's look at some important places the number three shows up in scripture. Please read Exodus 23:14-17. If your bible has a title for this section of scripture, write it here: _____

27. How many times a year were the men to go to Jerusalem to celebrate the Lord's Feasts? _____

CHAPTER 1 – PART I

28. Now look up and read Joshua 1:11. How many days did Joshua tell his officers it would be until they would cross the Jordan and enter the promised land?

   _____

29. Flip a few pages over to Joshua 2:16 and read it. How many days did Rahab tell the spies to hide? _____

30. Now read Daniel 3:19-24. How many Jews did King Nebuchadnezzar throw into the burning furnace? _____

31. Read Jonah 1:17. How many days and nights was Jonah in the fish's belly?

   _____

32. Matthew 12:40 clearly relates Jonah's story with Jesus' life. Please read it now. To what three days of Jesus' life was he referring in this passage? _____

   _____

33. The day after Jesus was crucified the chief priests and Pharisees went to Pilate and asked him to secure Jesus' tomb for a specific number of days. Please read that story in Matthew 27:62-64. How many days was it? _____

34. The chief priests and Pharisees were quoting Jesus in these verses. Let's look at the scripture where Jesus said what they quoted. Please read Mark 9:30.

35. Please read the story in John 2:13-19. When the Jews asked Him for a sign to validate His authority, how did Jesus answer them? (verse 19) _____

   _____

   _____

13

JUST JESUS

36. In Acts 2, Peter is trying to convince people that Jesus was who He said He was. Please read Acts 2:38-41. About how many thousand people accepted Jesus as their savior that day? _____

37. Please use your online bible study tool to find where else in scripture three is an important number, then list some of the places you find here. _____

_____

_____

_____

_____

_____

The number three or a reference to it appears over 450 times in scripture.

38. Is there anything you notice in common about the majority of the stories you've just read? _____

_____

39. What is amazing about the fact that the stories we are pointed to by John's mere mention of the number three are about more of Jesus' miracles? _____

_____

_____

CHAPTER 1 – PART I

40. In John 1:12, the disciple brings up the idea of God's children. How does he define a child of God? (pay attention to the dash right after verse 12)

_____

_____

_____

41. Why do you think he brings this up? _____

_____

_____

42. What does John tell us in John 1:14? _____

_____

_____

In John 1:14 our author just comes out and says it – no literary devices, no fluff. He simply says Jesus, though human, was the son of God. In verse 15, John reinforces his point that Jesus, as the son of God, has always existed by having John the Baptist say that "he existed long before me." So not only is John, the author, arguing that Jesus has always existed, he brings up a historical story where John the Baptist reaffirms that statement.

43. What do John 1:23, 31 and 34 tell us about what John the Baptist's role was?

_____

_____

_____

Jesus has always existed.

44. How is our role as believers similar to John the Baptist's? _____

_____

_____

_____

As believers our role is similar to that of John the Baptist. We are to testify that Jesus is the son of God.

JUST JESUS

45. Why might John have juxtaposed (placed side by side, in order to compare or contrast) John the Baptist baptizing with water next to Jesus baptizing with the Holy Spirit? _____

_____

_____

_____

_____

_____

46. In Isaiah 40:3 the prophet Isaiah told of someone who would come to prepare the way for the Christ. Who was that? _____

47. According to John 1:33, how was John the Baptist to know, of all the people he baptized, which ONE was the Messiah? _____

_____

_____

48. Who told him to look for that sign? _____

_____

CHAPTER 1 – PART I

49. Three other authors write about the same story, when God showed John the Baptist the sign He'd promised so he would know who His one and only son was. Please read the stories in Matthew 3:13-17, Mark 1:9-11 and Luke 3:21-22. In those stories, what was said when the spirit descended on Jesus after He was baptized by John the Baptist? _____

_____

_____

_____

"This is my Son, whom I love, with him I am well pleased."
—Matthew 3:17

50. Who said it? _____

51. Who heard it? _____

52. Summarize all you know about John the Baptist's role and what he was an eyewitness to regarding Jesus' baptism. _____

_____

_____

_____

_____

53. Do you think there was any doubt in John the Baptist's mind whether or not Jesus was the son of God? _____

_____

_____

JUST JESUS

Just as God told John the baptizer to watch for someone on whom a dove would descend and heaven would open up so he would be watchful, God told Israel to watch for a Messiah who would come and fulfill all the prophesies of the Old Testament. In a similar way, God tells us now as we wait for Jesus to come again to wait in expectation of Christ's return and all the while to be pointing others toward Him and proclaiming Jesus as Messiah.

Before Jesus came the first time, God told Israel to watch for a Messiah who would come and fulfill many prophecies of the Old Testament. As believers we are called to wait in expectation of Jesus' second coming, when He will fulfill the rest of the prophecies made about Him in scripture.

54. Is there any doubt in your mind that Jesus is the son of God? _____

_____

55. Take a minute to let the Holy Spirit take you back through your life and remind you of times when God told you in advance about something, then did it. Write those stories down and share them with someone this week. _____

_____

_____

_____

_____

_____

_____

56. What did John the Baptist do when he saw Jesus walking by in John 1:29-31?

_____

_____

57. When you recognize Jesus in your life, do you quickly share your stories about Jesus with those around you? _____

_____

_____

58. In proclaiming the Truth, John the Baptist was so convincing that two of his followers (Andrew and probably John, our author) immediately followed Jesus. What kind of reputation must John the Baptist have had? _____
_____

59. What kind of reputation do you have as a Jesus follower? _____
_____
_____
_____

60. Is there anything in your life that would keep others from following you into relationship with Jesus? _____
_____
_____
_____

61. Why do you think our author, John, left out Jesus' childhood and instead chose to begin his book about Jesus' life with Jesus' baptism, later in life?
_____
_____
_____
_____

What kind of reputation do you have as a Christ-follower?

John Chapter One – Part II

1. Spend some time listening to one of your favorite worship songs to get you focused on Jesus. Pray and ask God to teach you through His word as you study it. Ask Him to reveal hidden secrets and to open your eyes to what He wants you to learn in this time.

2. Please read John 1:35-51.

3. On another day, John the baptizer saw Jesus walking by and he again proclaimed unashamedly that Jesus was the Christ. What did he call Jesus in John 1:36?
   _____

4. Is there anything that keeps you from unashamedly proclaiming Jesus as the Christ? If so, what is it and why do you think that is? _____
   _____
   _____
   _____

> Jesus is
> "the Lamb of God."
> —John 1:36

5. What was the original word for the word translated, "lamb" in John 1:36?
   _____

6. What does that word mean? _____
   _____
   _____

7. Use your online study tool to help you find where else in the bible the word lamb was used.

   Old Testament uses of the word lamb: _____

   _____

   _____

   _____

   _____

   New Testament uses of the word lamb: _____

   _____

   _____

   _____

   _____

8. Do you find it interesting that the Old Testament words for lamb don't have any innocent or sacrificial connotations, while the New Testament words for lamb do? Why is that significant? _____

   _____

   _____

   _____

   _____

CHAPTER 1 – PART II

9. Do you find it interesting that the definition of the word translated, "lamb" in some Revelation verses carries a connotation of the lamb having pure intentions? Why is that important? _____

_____

_____

_____

10. What was the original word for the word that is translated, "of God" in John 1:36?? _____

11. What does that word mean? _____

_____

_____

_____

12. What is John the Baptist saying Jesus' relation to God is? _____

_____

_____

of God:

   Strong's number – G2316

   original word – theos

   meaning – God, the Supreme Divinity

13. How do you know when something "owns" you? List some positive consequences of being "owned". _____

_____

_____

_____

_____

JUST JESUS

14. Does God truly "own" you? What proof of that is there in your day to day life?

_____
_____
_____
_____
_____

15. If God doesn't "own" you right now, what does? _____

_____
_____

> If God truly "owns" you, what proof of that is there in your life? If God doesn't own you, what does?

16. When Jesus asked John and Andrew "what do you want" which can be translated, "what are you looking for" or "what do you seek?" in John 1:38, do you think Jesus was expecting them to answer, "We want to belong to God, like you do?" or "We want God to 'own' us too"? Or maybe, "We want you, Jesus"? If so, why didn't they answer His question? _____

_____
_____

17. What do you want most in the world? What are you seeking after?

_____
_____

18. What did Andrew and John ask Jesus (in John 1:38) instead of answering Him?

_____

CHAPTER 1 – PART II

19. Use your online bible study tool to help you find other verses in the New Testament that contain the word translated "abide" and list some here:

    _____

    _____

    _____

    _____

    _____

    _____

20. Where does Jesus abide? _____

21. Where are we to abide? _____

22. How did Jesus answer Andrew and John in John 1:39? _____

    _____

23. According to John 1:41, what was the first thing Andrew did after deciding to follow Jesus? _____

    _____

    _____

    _____

"Come …
and you will see."
—John 1:39

JUST JESUS

24. Have you recently shared your testimony with someone or told another person about an answered prayer or something God recently did in your life? If so, please share it here: _____

_____

_____

_____

_____

_____

25. What did Jesus do when Andrew brought his brother Simon to Him in John 1:42? _____

26. In this discourse, we can see God's invitation to us. What is His invitation?

_____

_____

_____

27. In John 1:43, what does Jesus tell Philip to do? _____

28. What did He mean by that? _____

_____

_____

_____

_____

Jesus wants us to spend time with Him because He wants to spend time with us.

"Follow me"
—Jesus

CHAPTER 1 – PART II

29. What does it mean for someone to "follow Christ"? _____

_____

_____

_____

_____

_____

30. Do people "follow" you in your relationship with Christ?_____

_____

_____

31. What does Philip do immediately after following Jesus? _____

_____

Jesus is a gentleman. He does not force anyone to follow Him, but He invites everyone to.

32. Did Jesus force people to follow Him? _____

33. If Jesus didn't force people to follow Him, do you think He wants us to try to convince people to have a relationship with Christ by using force? Why or why not? _____

_____

We can see Christ's invitation to eternal life here, but it's only an invitation, not a force. We have to choose to believe. The exchange between Jesus and Nathanael demonstrates our choice to believe or not.

_____

_____

_____

JUST JESUS

"You will see greater
things than that."

—John 1:50

34. What is the benefit that Jesus expounds on in John 1:50 and 51 for those who choose to believe He is the son of God? _____

_____

_____

_____

John Chapter Two

1. Spend some time listening to one of your favorite worship songs to get you focused on Jesus. Pray and ask God to teach you through His word as you study it. Ask Him to reveal hidden secrets and to open your eyes to what He wants you to learn in this time.

2. Please read John 2:1-25.

3. Why do you think a wedding is where Jesus performed His first public miracle?

   _____

   _____

   _____

4. Use your online bible study tool to learn about another important wedding in Revelation 19:7-9.

5. Now turn back to John 2. Had Mary, Jesus' mom, seen Jesus perform any miracles before she told Him at the wedding, "they have no more wine"?

   _____

   _____

6. How did Jesus respond to the need His mom made known to Him?

   _____

   _____

JUST JESUS

7. What does Jesus' question to His mom infer about Jesus' desire to do His mom's will versus doing His Heavenly Father's will? _____
_____
_____
_____

8. If you have children, do you ever try to push your will or agenda on your children over God's will for your children? If so, why do you think we do that?
_____
_____
_____

9. What direction did Mary give the servants regarding Jesus in John 2:5?
_____

"Do whatever He tells you."
—John 2:5

10. What does her statement say about her faith and about her knowledge of Jesus' character? _____
_____
_____
_____

11. Did Mary get her problem solved, even though she didn't offer Jesus any suggestions on how to do it? _____

12. When you ask Jesus to do something in your life, do you, like Mary, lay the problem at His feet and let Him decide how to handle it or do you also try to tell Him how He should solve your problem? Why do you think you do this?

   _____

   _____

   _____

   _____

13. What were the jars mentioned in John 2:6 used for? (Look this up in the NIV and KJV translations, please.) _____

14. What does Jesus turn the water into? _____

15. Would you say then that Jesus redeemed the water when He turned it into wine? _____

16. In the same way that we might ask, "Which is better, water or wine?", we can compare our life with Jesus to our life without Jesus and decide which is "better". Share some ways your life with Jesus is better than it was without Him.

   _____

   _____

   _____

   _____

   _____

17. What is the drink of communion? _____

18. What does it represent? _____

19. Keeping in mind that Jesus is the fulfillment of the old law, what does the water in the ceremonial jugs represent? _____

_____

_____

_____

_____

20. What does the wine represent? _____

_____

_____

21. What was the surprise when the servants took the new wine to the master of the wedding? _____

_____

_____

22. How is Jesus the better sacrifice for our sins? _____

_____

_____

23. Recap briefly how Jesus turning water into wine represents Jesus purifying or saving us from our sins. _____

_____

_____

_____

_____

24. In John 2:11 John tells us why Jesus performed signs and wonders. Why did He perform them? _____

Jesus performed miracles to reveal His glory to mankind.

25. The next section of scripture provides us another look at Jesus' redemptive power. Please read through John 2:12-23 with these "redemption" lenses on. How did Jesus redeem or purify the temple in these verses? _____

_____

_____

_____

26. Why would Jesus have scattered people from the temple this time, when He had not done so many other times He'd had the opportunity to? _____

_____

_____

_____

JUST JESUS

27. To whom or what is Jesus referring when He tells the Jews to "destroy this temple and I will raise it again in three days"? _____

28. Discuss the parallels between water being turned into wine, the temple being restored after being used as a market, and Jesus alluding to His body as the temple that would be restored after three days. _____

_____

_____

_____

_____

_____

29. Why is this significant in the book of John? _____

_____

_____

_____

_____

30. John 2:23 says, "many people saw the miraculous signs Jesus was doing". What did the people do as a result of seeing these signs? _____

_____

31. The last section of Chapter 2 is very interesting. Please read vs 23-25. What was Jesus in Jerusalem for? _____

CHAPTER 2

32. Please use your online study tool to learn more about what the Feast of Passover celebrates. Briefly summarize it here. _____

_____

_____

_____

_____

Passover:
An eight-day festival beginning on 15 Nisan that celebrates the deliverance of the Jewish people (Israel) from slavery in Egypt.

33. Why would John mention it here? _____

_____

_____

_____

_____

34. Use your online study tool to look up the original meaning of the word translated, "entrust" in John 2:24. What is the original word? What is Strong's number for it? _____

35. What does that word mean? _____

_____

_____

Entrusting:

Strong's number – G4100

original word – pisteuo

meaning – to believe, have faith, be committed to, to trust in.

*This word is used eighty-nine times in the book of John.

36. Why is it ironic that Jesus said He "would not entrust Himself to them, for He knew all men"? _____

_____

_____

_____

37. Using a concordance or your online study tool, find out how many times the word you looked up for question #34 is used in the book of John.

_____

38. Why is that significant? _____

_____

_____

_____

_____

39. In John 2:25 we learn that Jesus did not need man's testimony about Himself because Jesus knew what was in a man. What does that mean? What was the original word translated, "knew" in that verse? _____

_____

_____

_____

_____

It is interesting that Jesus did not entrust Himself to man before He died, but He did entrust mankind with continuing His mission while He is gone and until He comes back.

CHAPTER 2

40. What does it mean? _____

_____

_____

_____

41. What does it mean to you to know Jesus has first-hand knowledge of your heart, and He loves you anyway? _____

_____

_____

_____

Blueletterbible.org says the word translated, "knew", is ginosko in Greek. It means to come to recognize, perceive, to know especially through personal experience; to have first hand knowledge of. It is also a Jewish idiom for sexual intercourse between a man and a woman; to know intimately.

John Chapter Three

1. Spend some time listening to one of your favorite worship songs to get you focused on Jesus. Pray and ask God to teach you through His word as you study it. Ask Him to reveal hidden secrets and to open your eyes to what He wants you to learn in this time.

2. Please read John 3:1-36.

3. Use your online study tools to find out what a Pharisee was/is. Write it here:
   _____
   _____
   _____

4. Who did Nicodemus believe Jesus to be? (see John 3:2) _____
   _____
   _____

5. What do you think Jesus is trying to teach Nicodemus in John 3:3?
   _____
   _____
   _____
   _____

CHAPTER 3

While the original documents recording these stories were not divided into chapters, it's helpful for us to have them divided because it's easier for our minds to stay on track with smaller segments of scripture. However, it is interesting to note how intentional the author is in transitioning from the last segment to the next. He's just finished by saying that Jesus knows what is in a man and then, wham, he introduces us to a man named Nicodemus.

In doing so, the author reminds us of the comparison of Jesus, the son of God, to a mere man.

A Pharisee was a "do-er" who sought praise for his works or deeds.

JUST JESUS

When helping someone get to know Jesus, help them understand their need for a Savior.

6. What, then, might be the first step you could take in helping someone get into a relationship with Christ? _____
_____
_____

7. Please read John 3:5-8 again. What do you think Jesus is teaching Nicodemus in these verses? _____
_____
_____
_____

8. In John 3:8 Jesus supports His argument by talking about the wind. How much control did Nicodemus have over the wind, according to this verse? _____
_____

9. How much control is Jesus saying Nicodemus has in redeeming himself from his fallen state? _____
_____
_____

10. What is Jesus saying in these verses about God's ability to redeem and transform us, compared to our abilities or efforts? _____
_____
_____
_____

CHAPTER 3

11. In John 3:14 Jesus reminds Nicodemus of a story about the Israelites. You'll find this story in Numbers 21:7-9. Please read it now. What did God tell Moses to do in Numbers 21:8? _____
   _____

12. What did Moses and the people do in Numbers 21:9 and what was the result?
   _____
   _____
   _____

13. Apart from looking at the snake pole, is there anything the people did to get to live? _____

14. Who did the work, then, when people were healed from their snake bites?
   _____

15. Is there anything you can do to work your way into the kingdom? Who has to do the work? _____

16. Jesus pleads with Nicodemus in John 3:10-15. What does Jesus want Nicodemus to do? _____
   _____
   _____

> The snake raised up on Moses' pole is a symbol of Christ who was raised on the cross. In the same way that people who were bitten by a snake could look at the snake on Moses' pole and be saved, people who recognize their need for a Savior can look to Jesus to save them.

41

17. John 3:14 mentions the Son of Man being lifted up. What is that about and how is it related to the snake story we just read? _____

_____

_____

_____

_____

_____

> When helping someone get to know Jesus, help them understand there is nothing they can do to gain relationship with Jesus. They simply must believe.

18. With this in mind, what could our next step in helping introduce people to Jesus be? _____

_____

_____

_____

Jesus just finished telling Nicodemus (in vs 15) that anyone who believes in God's redemptive plan will have eternal life. In verse 16 He tells us the how and the why of that plan.

19. Please read John 3:16 and 17, keeping in mind who is saying the words. Stop and make yourself realize that Jesus is saying this about Himself. How does that make you feel? _____

_____

_____

CHAPTER 3

20. According to John 3:16, what motivated God to send us His one and only son?
_____

"For God so loved the world that He gave His one and only Son, that whoever believes in Him will not perish but have everlasting life."
— John 3:16

21. With this in mind, what could be our third step in helping introduce others to Jesus? _____
_____
_____
_____

When helping someone get to know Jesus, help them understand the benefits of knowing Jesus; the peace, sense of belonging, comfort, and relationship as well as getting to spend eternity with Him.

22. According to the beginning of John 3:17, what did God NOT send His son to do? _____

23. In the same verse He tells us what God DID send His son to do. What was that? _____
_____

God did not send His Son to condemn us. He sent Him to save us.

24. What do you think God thinks when the church uses Christ's teachings to condemn people? _____
_____

"God didn't go to all the trouble of sending his Son merely to point an accusing finger, telling the world how bad it was. He came to help, to put the world right again."
—John 3:17
The Message

25. How does the wording in the second part of John 3:17 reiterate that a person must first understand they need a savior before they will ever understand things of the kingdom? _____
_____
_____

26. Jesus pours His conviction out to Nicodemus in extra measure in John 3:18-21. Please read that segment now. According to these verses, who is NOT condemned? Who is already condemned? Why? _____

_____

_____

> "Whoever believes in him is not condemned, but whoever does not believe stands condemned . . . *because* they have not believed."
>
> —John 3:18, emphasis added

27. John 3:19-21 give us some insight into why people might choose to not believe. What is their reason? _____

_____

_____

28. Keeping in mind that one of the reasons people don't come into the light is because they are afraid their evil deeds will be exposed, should our conversations, as Christ's friends, ever be flavored with condemnation? _____

_____

_____

29. What might or conversations be flavored with instead? _____

_____

30. Please read John 3:22-27. Who is this argument between and what is it about?

_____

_____

CHAPTER 3

31. Why is it ironic that people are arguing about how they customarily purified themselves while Jesus is baptizing people nearby? _____

    _____

    _____

    _____

32. Why do you think John the Baptist's disciples were jealous that "everyone was going to (Jesus)" to be baptized instead of John? _____

    _____

    _____

33. Did John the Baptist take the bait? Please read John 3:27-36 to find out how he responded to his disciples, then summarize John the Baptizer's response in John 3:27-30 using your own words. _____

    _____

    _____

    _____

34. In John 3:31-36 we are back to hearing from John the Baptist. What does he call Jesus in verse 31 and to whom does he compare Him? _____

    _____

    _____

45

JUST JESUS

Jesus was no ordinary man. He was the Son of God, the Messiah (in Hebrew) the Christ (in Greek).

35. Remembering back to Chapter 1, what was John the Baptist (and what is John, our author) trying to convince people of? _____

    _____

    _____

36. What do the Johns tell us that God gives without limit in verse 34?

    _____

37. John the Baptist summarizes what Jesus was trying to teach Nicodemus (and us) earlier in this chapter. Please read John 3:35-36, then summarize it in your own words. _____

    _____

    _____

38. What, in a nutshell, could our line of reasoning be when we are trying to influence people (with whom we have earned the right to have the conversation) to start a relationship with Jesus? _____

    _____

    _____

John Chapter Four

1. Spend some time listening to one of your favorite worship songs to get you focused on Jesus. Pray and ask God to teach you through His word as you study it. Ask Him to reveal hidden secrets and to open your eyes to what He wants you to learn in this time.

2. Please read John 4:1-54.

3. Who was actually baptizing people in John 4:2? _____

4. Why do you think Jesus decided to go back to Galilee? _____
   _____
   _____

5. How do you think Jesus felt about His disciples when He was free to go to Galilee and knew the Gospel would continue to spread in Judea? _____
   _____
   _____

6. Look at a Key Places in John map to become familiar with Jesus' route from Judea through Samaria to Galilee. Using the mileage key on the map, if there is one, approximately how many days do you think it took Jesus to get to Galilee?
   _____

> Google "Key Places in the Book of John" to view maps of where the stories in John took place.

JUST JESUS

7. Do you think it's amazing that while on a two or three day, approximately 50-mile walk, Jesus walked up to a well at exactly the same time the Samaritan woman was at the well? _____

8. Are you able to recognize when God meets you in similar ways, at just the right time and place, in your life? If so, write a couple examples down.

   _____

   _____

   _____

   _____

9. According to John 4:5 who owned the land and who owned the well?

   _____

   _____

10. You may have noticed reading through the chapter of John 4, that there is a constant theme of redemption; redemption of the woman at well, and of the official's son. Joseph, the man who owned the land where the well was located, has an amazing redemption story of his own. Please read his story in Genesis chapters 37, 39-45. Eight chapters, I know, but it's a great story. You can do it!

11. Why is it important to notice that it's Joseph's land that the well is on, and why would I ask you to read Joseph's story in the middle of our study on the book of John? _____

    _____

    _____

Redemption: an act of redeeming or atoning for a fault or a mistake, the state of being redeemed; deliverance, rescue; atonement for guilt; repurchase, as of something sold; paying off, as of a mortgage, bond or note; recovery by payment, as of something pledged.[1]

CHAPTER 4

12. Let's go back to John 4 and start reading at verse 6. If you have a study bible, or notes in your bible on verse 6, please use them to find out what time "the sixth hour" means. _____

13. Remembering back to last week's homework, what three things can we do to help others get into relationship with Christ? _____

    _____
    _____
    _____
    _____
    _____
    _____

14. Now let's watch as Jesus uses these ideas and His physical need for water to show a Samaritan woman her spiritual need. Please read John 4:7-9.

15. What need does Jesus have? _____

16. Why was the Samaritan woman surprised Jesus asked her for a drink?

    _____
    _____
    _____
    _____

When helping someone get to know Jesus, help them understand:

1. their need for a Savior

2. there is nothing they can do to gain relationship with Jesus. They simply have to believe that He is who He says He is

3. the benefits of knowing Jesus; the peace, sense of belonging, comfort, and relationship as well as getting to spend eternity with Him

JUST JESUS

17. As a human, was there anything He could do to satisfy His thirst or did He have to rely on someone else loaning Him a cup and the water quenching His dry throat? _____
_____
_____

18. Now read John 4:10-15. What "offer" does Jesus make to the woman?
_____
_____
_____

19. What does the living water Jesus offered to the woman represent? _____
_____
_____
_____

For proof of God's fantastic sense of humor see John 4:12, 4:19-20, or 4:25-26.

20. God has an amazing sense of humor. Please read verse 12 again then write an alternate response you think Jesus might've wanted to give her. _____
_____
_____

21. Jesus changes the subject abruptly in verse 16. Please read John 4:16-20.

22. What is Jesus' point in verses 17 and 18? _____
_____

CHAPTER 4

23. Did you notice that just as the Samaritan woman can meet Jesus' need for water, Jesus can meet her need for a savior who can pull her out of her sinful life?

   _____

24. We find another instance of God's humor in verses 19-20. What is the woman trying to do here? _____

   _____

   _____

   _____

25. According to Jesus, in John 4:21-24, does God care much about where we worship? What kind of worshippers does the Father seek? _____

   _____

   _____

26. In John 4:25-26 we see God's humor again. What irony is presented in the fact that the Samaritan woman "knew the Messiah is coming" but didn't recognize Him when He was talking with her face to face? _____

   _____

   _____

   _____

27. Have you ever known someone (maybe you) who, from all looks and appearances, Jesus was standing right in front of, but who just couldn't see Him? If so, share your story here: _____

_____

_____

_____

_____

_____

_____

28. Why is it interesting that the first time Jesus clearly announces Himself as the Son of God (see verse 26) it's to a woman who needs redemption on the land of a son, Joseph, whose story is all about redemption? _____

_____

_____

_____

29. Please read John 4:27-30. What did the Samaritan woman do when Jesus' disciples came back? _____

_____

_____

CHAPTER 4

30. What did the Samaritan woman leave and why might this detail be significant?
_____
_____

31. Please read verses 31-38. What perceived need does Jesus have here?
_____

32. Considering that water and food are two of our most basic needs, is it interesting to you that Jesus uses these basic needs to teach us about our spiritual needs?
_____
_____

33. Does it make you feel better when you read things like verse 33 where Jesus' disciples had completely missed the point and had NO clue what He was talking about? _____

34. Why do you think God put examples of people missing the point in the Bible?
_____
_____

35. In verse 34 what does Jesus say one of His most basic needs is (His food)?
_____

36. What type of harvest is Jesus talking about in John 4:35? _____
_____

> "Open your eyes and look at the fields! They are ripe for harvest."
> — John 4:35

37. Think about the idea Jesus expresses in John 4:35-38, through spiritual lenses, and write it here in your own words. _____

_____

_____

_____

_____

_____

38. Please read John 4:39-42. Why did many people from the Samaritan woman's town believe initially? _____

_____

39. After that, what caused many more people to become believers?

_____

40. How can we use a similar approach to help others get to know Christ?

_____

_____

_____

_____

41. Please read John 4:43-45. What, according to John 2:23, had Jesus done at the Passover? _____

_____

CHAPTER 4

42. Use Google to learn about why so many people were in Jerusalem for the Passover Feast. Be careful to choose reliable websites from which to get your information. Write what you learn here: _____

_____

_____

_____

_____

> "A major category of Jewish holidays is the pilgrimage festival. Described in the Hebrew Bible as celebrating both agricultural festivals and historical events in the history of the Jewish people, these three holidays were set aside in biblical times for people to travel to the ancient Temple in Jerusalem. These three holidays are Pesach (Passover), Shavuot (Feast of Weeks), and Sukkot (Festival of Tabernacles)."[2]

43. According to the second part of John 4:45 why did the Galileans welcome Jesus? _____

_____

44. Please read verses 46-47. What kind of official was it whose son was sick?

_____

Go to https://chosenpeople.com/site/passover-in-israel-past-and-present/ to learn more about Passover in Jerusalem.

45. Looking at the Samaritan woman and this royal official, does Jesus cater to one "people group" over any other? _____

46. What people groups are we called to share Jesus with? _____

_____

47. What did the official ask Jesus to do? _____

_____

48. How did Jesus respond? _____

_____

JUST JESUS

49. What did Jesus tell the official in verse 50? _____

    _____

50. Did the official get to see the miracle happen? _____

51. Was the official's son healed? _____

52. Why, according to the second half of John 4:50, do you think that is?

    _____

    _____

> "The man took Jesus at his word."
> — John 4:50

53. Even though the official didn't see his son healed, he put two and two together and acknowledged his son was healed at exactly the moment Jesus said he would be healed. What happened as a result of the official sharing his "testimony" of this story with his whole household? _____

    _____

John Chapter Five

CHAPTER 5

1. Spend some time listening to one of your favorite worship songs to get you focused on Jesus. Pray and ask God to teach you through His word as you study it. Ask Him to reveal hidden secrets and to open your eyes to what He wants you to learn in this time.

2. Please read John 5:1-47.

3. What is the name of the pool in verse 2? _____

4. Use your online bible study tool to look that word up in its original form. What does Bethesda mean? What was special about this pool? _____

_____

_____

_____

> Go to https://www.gotquestions.org/Pool-of-Bethesda.html to learn more about the Pool of Bethesda.

5. According to verse 5, how many years had a certain invalid been in his condition? _____

6. If the pool you were laying by had special healing powers, would you expect to have been healed in thirty-eight years? _____

7. What does Jesus ask the man in verse 6? _____

_____

> "Do you want to get well?"
> —John 5:6

JUST JESUS

8. How does the man reply? (see verse 7) _____

_____

_____

9. How does Jesus respond to his excuses in John 5:8? _____

_____

_____

10. According to verse 9, how long did it take the invalid to be cured, pick up his mat and walk? _____

11. Was Jesus' ability to heal the invalid at all affected by the fact that he did not know who Jesus was, and that he had not asked Him to heal him?

_____

12. What do the Jews call Jesus in John 5:12? _____

13. Going back to the beginning of our study on the book of John, what is one of the main things John is trying to teach people through these writings?

_____

_____

14. What does Jesus say about Himself in verse 17 that affirms He is no ordinary man? (John restates it in verse 18 in case we missed it.) _____

_____

Jesus was not your run-of-the-mill, ordinary "fellow". He was the Son of God.

CHAPTER 5

15. Please read John 5:19-27 making note of how many times the words Father or Son are used. How many times is the word, "Father" used in these verses? How many times is the word "Son" used? _____

_____

_____

16. So together, in those nine verses, how many times are the words "father" or "son" used? _____

17. What is the significance of those words? What argument is the author using them to support? _____

_____

_____

18. Who, according to verse 22, is the judge, the Father or the Son? _____

19. What does the second part of John 5:23 say? _____

_____

_____

20. Considering that verse, what might you suggest to someone who says there are many ways to God? _____

_____

_____

_____

The words, "father" or "son" are used eighteen times in John 5:19-27 in order to establish that Jesus was the Son of God.

21. In verse 24 Jesus repeats what He taught Nicodemus a couple of chapters earlier. What is the gist of this teaching? _____

_____

_____

_____

22. What four testimonies does Jesus mention in John 5:31-37? _____

_____

_____

_____

23. Verses 37 and 38 further explain that Jesus is the only way to God. What do they say? _____

_____

_____

24. Please read John 5:39-40. According to Jesus, what did the Jews think would bring them eternal life? _____

25. What does Jesus say the meat of those scriptures is? _____

_____

_____

CHAPTER 5

26. Restate, in your own words, what Jesus said to the Jewish people in John 5:39-40. _____
_____
_____
_____

27. Look back to John 1:1. What is Jesus called in that verse? _____

28. How is Jesus comparing and contrasting Himself as the only Savior able to give the Jewish people eternal life with the Law or Word that they are trying to use to gain it? _____
_____
_____

29. Who is the Jew's accuser and on whom were their hopes set, according to John 5:45? _____

30. Who wrote the first five books of the bible; Genesis, Exodus, Leviticus, Numbers and Deuteronomy, which comprised the scriptures the Jewish people were counting on to get them eternal life? _____

31. Why might we, as followers of Christ, be thankful for the gift of the Torah the Jewish people left us? (think of the scriptures as the law) _____
_____
_____

The Torah, or the Law as it is sometimes referred as, is made up of the first five books of the bible; Genesis, Exodus, Leviticus, Numbers and Deuteronomy.

JUST JESUS

32. In John 5:46 Jesus tells the Jews that Moses wrote about Him. Let's look at what Moses wrote. Please read Genesis 3:15. To whom does the word, "he" near the end of the verse, refer? _____

33. Now let's look back to John 5:47. Did the Jewish people believe what Moses had written about Jesus? _____

34. How is Jesus once again juxtaposing (comparing and contrasting) Himself with the scriptures or law when He asks, "if you didn't believe what Moses wrote about Me, how are you going to believe what I say?" Explain. _____

_____

_____

_____

35. Were the Jews Jesus was talking to believers? _____

36. Which do you think Jesus would have preferred? (circle one)

    a) The Jews keep studying the scriptures to understand them?

    b) The Jews stop studying their scriptures so much (besides, they were meant to point them to Christ, not to fill them with knowledge) and just spend some time with Him?

37. To which option do you think it is better for us to direct our friends?

_____

_____

CHAPTER 5

38. How effective is it for us to tell our friends to read the bible when they haven't even decided if they believe Jesus is who He says He is? Why is this not very effective? _____

_____

_____

39. How can we personally be Jesus to our friends who don't yet know Him, so they can "just spend some time with Him"? _____

_____

_____

_____

_____

John Chapter Six

1. Spend some time listening to one of your favorite worship songs to get you focused on Jesus. Pray and ask God to teach you through His word as you study it. Ask Him to reveal hidden secrets and to open your eyes to what He wants you to learn in this time.

2. Please read John 6:1-71.

3. Please look at a Key Places in John map to familiarize yourself with where Jesus travels between Ch 5 and 6, from Jerusalem to the far side of the Sea of Galilee. Approximately how far was that? _____

4. According to John 6:2, why were crowds of people following Jesus?
   _____
   _____

5. Use your online bible study tool to learn the original meaning of the word translated "signs" in the NIV, in verse 2. What was the original word? What did it mean?
   _____
   _____
   _____
   _____

Google "Key Places in the Book of John" to view maps of where the stories in John took place.

JUST JESUS

6. Considering that definition, why do you think our author, John, used the word "sign" instead of "miracle" in his writing to us? _____

_____

_____

_____

_____

_____

> The signs Jesus performed were that by which Jesus distinguished Himself from others. His signs proved He was no ordinary man. He was the Son of God.

7. What does the Jewish Passover Feast celebrate? _____

_____

_____

_____

_____

> Go to https://www.gotquestions.org/what-is-Passover.html to learn more about the Feast of Passover.

8. Please read John 6:5-9, then compare and contrast Philip's response (see verse 7) with Andrew's response (see verse 9). _____

_____

_____

_____

_____

_____

_____

9. When God places a need in front of you, do you most often respond like Philip with a statement of little to no faith, or like Andrew with a question and at least a hint of faith? Why do you think that is? _____

_____

_____

_____

_____

10. How much food did Jesus have to work with? _____

_____

11. What adjective is used to describe the loaves of bread and the fish? _____

12. Do you see how the author is telling us, "they don't have much to work with here"? _____._____

13. How does Jesus respond to Andrew's mustard-seed-size faith? (see verse 10)

_____

14. According to John 6:10 how many people were there? _____

15. What additional information does Matthew give us about this crowd in Matthew 14:21? _____

_____

_____

Jesus fed over five thousand men (not to mention women and children) with five small loaves of bread and two small fish. And He had twelve baskets of bread left over.

JUST JESUS

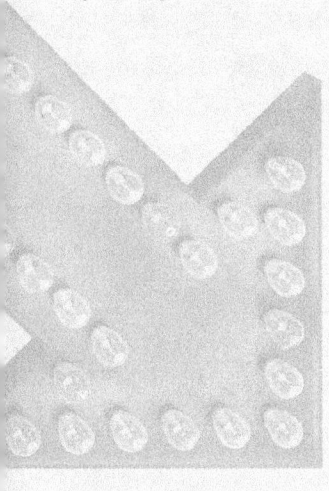

16. What did Jesus do before He started distributing the bread? _____

    _____

    _____

17. Was Jesus stingy in the portions of bread and fish He gave out?

    _____

18. What did Jesus have His disciples do in verse 12? _____

    _____

19. How many baskets were filled with the left-over bread? _____

20. How many disciples still needed to eat (all of them, they'd been serving up to this point)? _____

21. How many and what type loaves of bread had they started with?

    _____

22. Who did the people say Jesus was, according to John 6:14? _____

    _____

    _____

23. Does your bible have a note on John 6:14? If so, go to and reference the verse here. _____

CHAPTER 6

24. What do Deuteronomy 18:15 and 18 say? _____

   _____

   _____

   _____

   _____

25. What does Deuteronomy 18:19 go on to say? _____

   _____

   _____

26. How do these words reinforce what our author John has been trying to convince us of in the first five chapters of his book? _____

   _____

   _____

   _____

   _____

27. Please read John 6:16-24. Write a brief summary of what happened here.

   _____

   _____

   _____

   _____

   _____

   _____

JUST JESUS

> The crowd asked Jesus, "when did you get here" when Jesus got to Capernaum, but I think what they really wanted to ask Him was, "HOW did you get here."

28. How many miles had the disciples rowed before Jesus came to their aid? Why is that an important number to us? _____
_____

29. What did the crowd ask Jesus once they found Him in Capernaum?
_____
_____

30. Did Jesus answer their question? What did He say about their motives for following Him? _____
_____
_____
_____

31. What food is Jesus talking about in John 6:27? _____
_____

32. Verse 27 is often cross referenced with John 6:54. Please read that verse now. What is the food Jesus is offering them? _____
_____

33. What are the first three words in John 6:27? _____
_____

34. What are the last three words in that same sentence? _____
_____

CHAPTER 6

35. Why might the crowd's question in verse 28 make you think they aren't listening very carefully? _____

_____

_____

_____

36. What is the only work they need to do, according to verse 29?

_____

_____

> "Believe in the one he has sent."
> —John 6:29

37. Please read John 6:30–40. If Jesus had responded in His flesh, how do you think He might have answered their questions in verse 30? _____

_____

_____

_____

38. I love the irony of their commentary in John 6:31. What "news" did they share with Jesus in that verse? _____

_____

_____

_____

JUST JESUS

39. How does Jesus expound on the news they've just given Him? _____

40. How does Jesus define the bread of God in John 6:33? _____

41. How does Jesus even more plainly define this bread in John 6:35? _____

42. What promise does Jesus make to anyone who believes in Him in verse 37?

"Whoever comes to me I
will never drive away."

—John 6:37

43. According to verses 39 and 40, what is God's will? _____

44. Were there any people groups left out in verse 40? _____

_____

_____

45. Does your life testimony bear witness to that verse or have you at times excluded certain people from the "everyone" He is talking about? _____

_____

_____

46. What were the Jews grumbling about in John 6:41? _____

_____

_____

47. How did Jesus respond to their grumblings in verse 48? _____

_____

48. Envision Jesus saying these words. What might He be doing with His hands when He says verses 50 and 51? _____

_____

_____

49. What does Jesus predict in the second half of verse 51? _____

_____

_____

CHAPTER 6

"My Father's will is that everyone who looks to the Son and believes in him will have eternal life."

—John 6:40

JUST JESUS

"We have been made holy through the sacrifice of the body of Jesus Christ once for all."
—Hebrews 10:10

50. Hebrews 10:10 is a cross reference for John 6:51. Please read that verse now. According to the Hebrews verse, through what sacrifice have we been made holy? _____
_____

51. According to Hebrews 10:10, is any other sacrifice necessary to make anyone who believes in Jesus holy? _____
_____
_____

52. What, according to John 6:52, did the Jews argue about at this point?
_____
_____
_____

53. Keeping in mind all the rules around what Jews could and couldn't eat, how offensive must this discourse have been to the Jewish people with whom Jesus was talking? _____

54. Please read John 6:52-59. Note how many times John uses the words, "eat" or "feeds on" in these verses. _____

55. If you happen to know from previous studies, what does the number seven often represent in scripture? _____

CHAPTER 6

56. What point is John, our author, making by using the words "eat" or "feeds on" seven times in this paragraph? _____
_____
_____

57. Jesus directly confronts His disciples' grumbling with a question in John 6:61. What does He ask them? _____
_____
_____

58. How does Jesus go on in John 6:62-63 to say that He had been speaking allegorically? _____
_____
_____

> By using the words "eat" or "feeds" seven times in John 6:52-59, John is confirming that Jesus' sacrifice was perfect. It was a once, for all solution to our need for a Savior.

59. God's timing is perfect. After I finished writing this chapter, I opened my email and found this, sent to me from Rabbi Grossbaum, a leader in my town's Jewish community. Please read it, keeping in mind the lesson we are doing.

> Dear Shelly,
>
> Modern society has given rise to an unprecedented level of wealth, convenience and technology. But with it has arrived unprecedented levels of aimlessness, anxiety and depression. Today we have the best access to water, nutritious food and medical care than any previous generation. Almost every place in the world is better off today than it ever was. And that's not all, in addition to all the basic needs, we have luxuries too!
>
> But one of the most important things are missing, something that is just as important as our physical needs: Nourishment for our souls. While we're so busy making sure we have the latest iPhone, we're neglecting to ensure that

our soul has it's basic sustenance cared for. We're so concerned with keeping up with the latest styles and trends that we've become spiritually anorexic. "Man does not live by bread alone, but rather by, whatever comes forth from the mouth of the L-rd does man live." This declaration by Moses (recorded in this week's Torah portion) is the cure to what ails modern society. The physical world, and all it provides, is not enough to sustain human life. Yes, with proper food and drink we'll be physically alive; yes, modern luxuries will provide a measure of comfort and some fleeting pleasure. But none of it will fill the gaping hole in our lives. This can only be accomplished by living a life that is spiritually in tune, too. However, instead of living a spiritually nourished life, many are afraid they'll gain too many spiritual "pounds." They think that it will dampen their physical pleasure to engage in Torah study or to fulfill additional Mitzvot. They don't want anyone to think that they are becoming a religious nut, G-d forbid.

So they remain on their dangerously low spiritual diet; once a year synagogue services, no more than basic Hebrew School education - and maybe a Jewish cultural reference, occasionally. But the truth is that life needs many ingredients, physical and spiritual. And overdosing on the physical doesn't diminish the need for the spiritual; in fact, it makes the need all the more urgent. Today is a perfect day to assess your spiritual calorie intake, take some time and analyze your life and determine where more G-dliness and spirituality can be incorporated.

Shabbat shalom![3]

60. Bonus question: Where are the verses the Rabbi quoted from Moses located in the bible? _____

61. In our consumer-centered world, how is your spiritual diet and what are you doing daily to nourish your soul? _____

_____

_____

How is your spiritual diet? What are you doing daily to nourish your soul?

John Chapter Seven

1. Spend some time listening to one of your favorite worship songs to get you focused on Jesus. Pray and ask God to teach you through His word as you study it. Ask Him to reveal hidden secrets and to open your eyes to what He wants you to learn in this time.

2. Please read John 7:1-52.

3. In the second chapter of John, Jesus went up to Jerusalem to celebrate the Lord's Feast called Passover. Use your online study tools (or look back at your Chapter 2 homework, question #32) to remind yourself what the Passover Feast commemorates. Write your notes here: _____

   _____

   _____

   _____

4. Much of John, Chapter 2 echoes that same theme of redemption. Here, in Chapter 7, Jesus goes secretly to the Lord's Feast of Tabernacles. Using your online tool, find out what the Lord's Feast of Tabernacles celebrates and commemorates. How long did this feast last? _____

   _____

   _____

Go to https://chosenpeople.com/site/feast-tabernacles/ to learn about the Feast of Tabernacles, also known as Sukkot.

Notice that in our previous chapter, 6, Jesus provides for the five thousand with a few fish and a couple loaves of bread. Then later in the chapter, He refers to Himself as the "bread of life", the ultimate provision for man's need. In Chapter 7, our author places this "provision" theme of Chapter 6 right next to the Feast of Tabernacles, which commemorates God's provision for Israel as they wandered in the desert by revealing Jesus as that provision. That's huge, but the Feast of Tabernacles represents much more than that, as we will see.

5. Please read John 7:1-13 and let your mind envision the scene as it unfolds, then summarize it in your own words. _____

_____

_____

_____

_____

_____

6. According to verse 4, what did Jesus' brothers think Jesus wanted to become? And what, according to Jesus' brothers, did public figures NOT do?

_____

_____

7. What do we learn in verse 5? _____

_____

8. According to John 7:11-13, what was the talk of the town about? _____

   _____

   _____

9. How did the Jews refer to Jesus in these same verses? _____

   _____

10. Why is it significant that our author, John, included those words?

    _____

    _____

    _____

11. Keeping in mind that the Feast of Tabernacles lasts for seven days, how many days did Jesus "act in secret"? (see verse 14) _____

12. How did Jesus reveal His secret? _____

    _____

13. What does Jesus say about His teaching in John 7:16-20? _____

    _____

    _____

14. At whom do you think Jesus may have been looking and specifically teaching when He spoke the words He did in verse 18? _____

    _____

    _____

CHAPTER 7

"Even his own brothers did not believe in him."
—John 7:5

"My teaching is not my own. It comes from the one who sent me."
—John 7:16

15. How does Jesus define a "public figure" in verse 18? _____

_____

_____

16. What additional plea does Jesus make to His brothers in verse 18?

_____

_____

_____

_____

17. What miracle is Jesus referring to in verse 21? (verse 23 may help you)

_____

_____

18. Look closely at verses 28-29. How many times does Jesus refer to Himself in these verses? (look for me, I, my, etc.) List them here. _____

_____

_____

19. How many times does Jesus refer to God? (look for he, him) Please list them here. _____

_____

_____

20. What do you think our author's point is in this discourse? _____

_____

_____

21. How does John 7:33 reinforce this idea of Jesus as a nomad? _____

_____

_____

_____

22. How are followers of Christ "nomads" in this world? _____

_____

_____

23. If you envision living as a nomad, what would your world look like and how would it be different from what it is now? _____

_____

_____

24. In verse 37 Jesus brings up living water. What does that verse say?

_____

_____

_____

For the first six days of the Feast of Tabernacles, or Sukkot, "The time of our joy", there were nightly water-drawing celebrations where the priests took a jug of water from the pool of Siloam and, after an elaborate processional up the hill, joyfully

---

CHAPTER 7

In your research on The Feast of Tabernacles, you probably learned that in addition to celebrating the harvest and God's provision for Israel, this feast also reminded each generation that their forefathers had wandered in the desert, living as nomads in temporary dwellings for forty years. In verse 28, Jesus shows Himself as a nomad. Just as Israel wandered in the desert because God sent them there (they were not there on their own accord), Jesus was here because God sent Him and He was not here on His own accord.

"On the last and greatest day of the festival, Jesus stood and said in a loud voice, 'Let anyone who is thirsty come to me and drink.'"

—John 7:37

poured it out on the rock on which the temple was built. Jewish tradition says the water was poured on the altar after the sacrifices were made. Some scholars believe pouring the water symbolized Israel's hope for future rain to produce abundant harvests, which is interesting when you think of the joy we can have now and the hope we have for our future because of Christ.

25. On the last day of the Feast, because it was a Sabbath, the priests did not make the journey to the pool, and therefore did not pour the water out on the rock of the temple mount. So, on the last day of the Feast, there would have been no water in the priests' ritual. According to John 7:37, on which day did Jesus teach about living water? _____

26. Discuss the possibility, or maybe even probability that Jesus spoke these words about living water "loudly" at the very moment the priests would normally have "joyfully" poured their jugs of water onto the stone of the temple mount.

_____
_____
_____
_____

27. Why is that significant? _____
_____
_____
_____

28. Please read Exodus 17:1-6 as well as Numbers 20:2. What are these verses about? _____
_____
_____

29. What does our author explain to us regarding what Jesus was really talking about when He said in John 7:38, "streams of living water will flow from within him"? _____
_____
_____
_____

30. Please read John 7:45-50. Were the chief priests and Pharisees happy with the temple guards when they got back to them? Why or why not? _____
_____
_____

31. We met Nicodemus in John Chapter 3. How does his question in John 7:51 reveal the hypocrisy of his fellow chief priests and Pharisees? _____
_____
_____
_____

> Just as God provided the water the Israelites needed as they wandered in the desert for forty years, in our current story in the book of John, God provided what they needed at that point, a Savior, namely, Jesus the Christ.

CHAPTER 7

32. How do the chief priests and Pharisees respond to Nicodemus? _____

_____

_____

_____

33. When someone in the faith lovingly rebukes your behavior, do you accept their counsel or do you, as the Pharisees and chief priests did here, quickly change the subject? _____

_____

_____

John Chapter Eight

1. Spend some time listening to one of your favorite worship songs to get you focused on Jesus. Pray and ask God to teach you through His word as you study it. Ask Him to reveal hidden secrets and to open your eyes to what He wants you to learn in this time.

2. Please read John 8:1-59.

3. Now let's take a closer look at the chapter in sections, starting with verses 1-11. Please re-read that now.

4. Where, according to John 8:1, did Jesus go? _____

5. Why'd Jesus go there and why alone? What are your thoughts? _____
   _____
   _____
   _____

6. There's a mini soap opera in John 8:3-11. Please read it now. What's the plot of this episode? _____
   _____
   _____
   _____

What's really going on here is that the teachers of the law and Pharisees are trying to trap Jesus so they can have Him arrested. In verse 5 they bring up the law, (this

---

The Mount of Olives was a mountain that was about 2,700 feet high. Its summit commanded amazing views of the city of Jerusalem and especially of the temple. When I study the bible, I like to try to picture the stories in my head. I wonder why Jesus went to the Mount of Olives. Did He just sit there looking down at the temple, with all the people who were trying to trap Him wandering aimlessly throughout it? Or, which is more akin to His character, did He sit there and pray for those same people? Was He thinking about the next day and what He was going to do in that temple area?

behavior requires stoning) which, if Jesus doesn't follow, could be cause for His arrest.

7. How does Jesus react to them trying to trap Him? _____

_____

_____

_____

8. How does Jesus' response to his questioners demonstrate that He is keeping the "law of Moses" mentioned in John 8:5? _____

_____

_____

_____

9. I can hardly read the story without envisioning the scene. Scripture doesn't tell us what Jesus wrote on the ground, but it's fun to speculate. What do you think He was writing? _____

_____

_____

10. Who, according to John 8:9, were the first to drop their stones and go away?

_____

_____

11. How have you gotten wiser with age? _____

_____

12. Who, besides the woman, was the only person left standing? _____

13. Who was the only person in the group who met the criteria listed in verse 7, "if any of you is without sin, let him be the first to throw a stone"? _____

While Jesus was the only one with the "right" to throw a stone at the woman, He chose not to. Instead, He showed her grace. In verses 10 and 11 Jesus and the woman share a sweet conversation. Picture the scene as you read through it once more.

14. Might Jesus have startled the woman when He asked her "where are they" in verse 10, because until that point she may have had her eyes closed or covered, readying herself to be stoned? Discuss. _____

_____

_____

_____

_____

15. How does Jesus respond to her sin? _____

_____

_____

> "Neither do I condemn you."
> —John 8:11

The rest of John 8 is divided in the NIV into sections titled, "The Validity of Jesus' Testimony", "The Children of Abraham", "The Children of the Devil" and "The Claims of Jesus About Himself". Two sections are about who Jesus says He is (God's child) and two are about other types of children. The author's point and Jesus' point are the same here – Jesus is defining Himself as God's Son and is contrasting Himself with Abraham's children and the Devil's children.

16. In John 8:12 Jesus says, "I am the light of the world" and He follows this with nine more, "I ams" in the following seventeen verses. Note each occurrence of "I am" in John 8:13-30. What do you think Jesus is trying to tell us about who He is?

_____

_____

_____

_____

_____

17. Verse 19 demonstrates that Jesus' audience just wasn't getting it. What did they ask Him here? _____

18. How does Jesus reply in the end of the same verse? _____

_____

_____

_____

19. Why do you think John tells us, in verse 20, where Jesus was when He said this? _____

_____

_____

20. John 8:23 is a fun one; just as the different sections in this chapter allow Jesus to compare Himself as the child of God to the children of Abraham and the devil, in this verse He compares Himself to His Jewish audience. Make a small table of who Jesus is, compared to who the Jews are.

Jesus is reiterating what He's been saying all along, that in order to know God you have to believe that Jesus is the son of God, that He died and rose again to forgive the sins of all mankind, and that He will return again someday to live with us for all eternity.

CHAPTER 8

21. Verse 24 hits us with a heavy punch. Please read it now. What does Jesus say will happen if someone does not believe that Jesus is who He is claiming to be?

    _____

    _____

22. Who was Jesus claiming to be at this point? _____

23. Please read John 8:25 again. What question do the Jews ask Jesus?

    _____

24. If you were Jesus in this scene, how would you have wanted to reply to them?

    _____

    _____

    _____

25. Instead, how does Jesus respond to their question? _____

    _____

    _____

26. Please read John 8:27-30 and think about whether or not you could say those same words about your own life. Could you? Why or why not? _____

    _____

    _____

    _____

JUST JESUS

27. Are you who you claim to be? Do you do anything on your own fruition? Do you speak only what God tells you? Do you know that God is with you and that He has not left you alone? Do you always do what pleases God? _____

_____

_____

_____

_____

_____

28. If you answered "no" to any of those questions, welcome to the gang. What can you do to become more like Jesus in that regard? _____

_____

_____

_____

_____

_____

29. There's a lot going on in the next section of scripture. Please read John 8:31-33. To whom is Jesus speaking, according to verse 31? _____

_____

30. What does Jesus say proves they are truly His disciples? _____

_____

_____

"If you hold to my teaching, you are really my disciples."

—John 8:31

31. If they hold to His teaching, what will the result be? _____
   _____
   _____

32. How do they respond in verse 33? _____
   _____
   _____

The Jews had always tried to earn their way to God by obeying His laws and following His commandments (or at least that's what they thought they were supposed to do to get to God). Here, Jesus is saying that the Old Covenant Laws that they thought gave them relationship with God have actually enslaved them and that only by believing in Jesus will they be truly free and have relationship with God.

33. Please read John 8:34-36 carefully a couple of times. According to verse 34 if you sin, what are you? _____

34. Does a slave have a permanent place in the family? _____

35. How long does a son belong to the family? _____

36. Do you know anyone who once confessed Jesus as Lord but who is not actively following Him now? _____

> "Then you will know the truth, and the truth will set you free."
> —John 8:32

Are you a slave to sin?

> When someone's son dies, does he stop being their son? No – his parents would still refer to him as "our son" even though he isn't around any longer. The same idea is true for spiritual children of God. Once a person has joined God's family, he or she is a child of God for all eternity. Period.

37. What promise of hope does verse 35 offer to you and to the person you had in mind in #36? _____

_____

_____

_____

38. What does Jesus mean in John 8:36 when He says, "if the Son sets you free, you will be free indeed?" _____

_____

_____

39. There are a few fun word plays going on in John 8:37-41. Let's look at them closely together. Please read those verses now.

    When Jesus says, "I know you're Abraham's descendants" He is chastising the Jews for not behaving the way Abraham's true children would. He's basically saying, "I know you call yourselves Abraham's kids, but you sure aren't acting like them." The Jews obviously got His "poke" because they respond in verse 39 with an emphatic, "Abraham is our father". Jesus uses the opportunity to explain Himself in verses 39-40, when He says, "if you were Abraham's children, then you would do the things Abraham did". He goes on in verse 40 to say, you're trying to kill Me and I haven't even done anything wrong/sinned. In other words, Abraham's kids would know the Old Testament law that says "do not murder" but you're trying to get Me killed. You're hypocrites.

40. Please read Hebrews 11:8, 9, 11, and 17 and write down how each verse begins.

    _____

41. How did Abraham do things and therefore, how would Abraham's children supposedly have done things? _____

42. What do we learn in Romans 4:3 that supports that truth? _____
   _____
   _____
   _____

43. What is Jesus trying to get the Jews in our story to understand and what is John, our author, trying to get his readers to understand here? _____
   _____
   _____
   _____

44. In John 8:41, Jesus starts a heated discussion. What does Jesus say in this verse?
   _____
   _____

45. What father is He talking about in this verse? (he defines it later in verse 44)
   _____

46. The Jews' rude protest is hot and may have burned deep into Jesus' soul. What did they say in verse 41? _____
   _____

CHAPTER 8

By faith <u>your name here</u> . . .

"Abraham believed God, and it was credited to him as righteousness."
—Romans 4:3

47. Have you ever wondered how often Jesus had been teased, scorned or even shunned for being an "illegitimate" child, born to a woman and man who hadn't had sex to create Him? How much flak do you think He took about that throughout His lifetime, and especially once He started to claim to be God's son? _____

_____

_____

48. Why is it ironic that the Jews conclude their argument with Jesus with the statement, "the only father we have is God Himself"? _____

_____

_____

_____

49. Do you think they may have been taunting Jesus, since He'd been saying that He was the son of God repeatedly? _____

50. Or do you think the Jews were actually that clueless and Jesus may have wanted to grab them and shake them in frustration, knowing they were so stuck in their own preconceptions about who He was that they really hadn't heard what He'd been saying? _____

CHAPTER 8

51. Please read John 8:42-47 and summarize it in your own words here.

   _____

   _____

   _____

   _____

   _____

   _____

   _____

52. I think Paul gives us a better summary of what John is saying here in 1 Corinthians 2:14. Please read that verse now, then summarize it here: _____

   _____

   _____

   _____

   _____

   _____

> "The person without the Spirit does not accept the things that come from the Spirit of God but considers them foolishness, and cannot understand them because they are discerned only through the Spirit."
>
> —1 Corinthians 2:14

53. Please read John 14:16-17 and 14:26. Why could the Jews not understand what Jesus was saying about Himself? _____

   _____

   _____

54. Let's go back and look at a verse that's so important I don't want us to miss it. Please re-read John 8:46.

    In asking this question, Jesus portrays Himself as someone with a clear conscience. Think, for a minute, how completely opposite that is of you and me. Yet, because of what Jesus did for us on the cross, we can live with an equally clear conscience. Imagine that.

55. Please read John 8:48-59, noting what two words Jesus uses to both begin and end His dialogue in these verses. (focus on verses 49 and 58) _____

56. The NIV translation tells us that "the earliest manuscripts and many other ancient witnesses do not have John 7:53-8:11", which means that Chapter 8 could, theoretically, begin with verse 12. Go back to that verse and see what words Jesus' testimony about Himself begins with. What were they? _____

57. If we omit the story about Jesus showing the adulterer grace and allow Chapter 8 to start with verse 12, this chapter begins and ends with Jesus saying, "I am". The "I AM" of the Old Testament (see Exodus 3:14) is the same "I AM" of the New Testament that shows up nearly twenty times in the book we are studying. Please look up as many of them as you feel led to:

    - Exodus 3:14

    - John 4:26

    - John 6:35, 41, 48, 51

    - John 8:12, 24, 28, 58

    - John 10:7, 9, 11, 14

"I AM WHO I AM"
—Exodus 3:14

CHAPTER 8

- John 11:25

- John 13:19

- John 14:6

- John 15:1, 5

- John 18:5-6, 8

58. Why would our author include these words of Jesus so many times in his writing to us? _____

_____

_____

59. What does Jesus' name, "I AM" mean to you personally? Who and what "is He" to you? _____

_____

_____

_____

60. When you want to help introduce someone to Christ, do you mention who Jesus is based on scripture or who He is to you, personally? Which have you found is more effective? _____

_____

_____

"I am … the bread of life, the light of the world, the gate, the good shepherd, the resurrection and the life, the way and the truth and the life, the true vine"

—Jesus

John Chapter Nine

1. Spend some time listening to one of your favorite worship songs to get you focused on Jesus. Pray and ask God to teach you through His word as you study it. Ask Him to reveal hidden secrets and to open your eyes to what He wants you to learn in this time.

2. Please read John 9:1-41.

3. Let's take this apart a bit, starting with John 9:1-12. When did Jesus encounter the blind man? _____
_____

4. According to verse 2, what incorrect teaching had Jesus' disciples believed?
_____
_____

5. How do we know this was false teaching? _____
_____
_____
_____

6. According to verse 4 whose responsibility is it to "do the work of Him who sent (Jesus)"? _____

7. What repeated "I am" statement do we find in John 9:5? _____
_____

"As long as it is day, we must do the works of him."
—John 9:4

JUST JESUS

8. Where did we first see this "I am" statement and what was it? _____

_____

_____

9. How are we, as followers of Christ, the light of the world? _____

_____

_____

_____

_____

10. What does Jesus do right after He defines Himself as the light of the world?

_____

_____

_____

11. What are we supposed to do as the light of the world? (see question #6)

_____

_____

_____

CHAPTER 9

12. Picture the scene in John 9:6-7, keeping in mind that the man was blind, so he himself couldn't see Jesus spitting in the dirt. Do you think Jesus did it quietly, or did He somehow let the man know exactly what He was doing?

_____

_____

_____

13. Do you think onlookers "ewed" in disgust and explained Jesus' actions as He mixed His saliva into mud? _____

14. Do we hear any protest at all from the blind man? _____

15. After Jesus put His homemade remedy on the man's eyes, what did Jesus say?

_____

16. What did the blind man do? _____

_____

17. What was the result of his obedience? _____

_____

18. If the way Jesus chooses to heal you doesn't look exactly how you think it should, for instance, He uses spit and dirt to heal you, will you complain or will you willingly do what Jesus tells you to do? _____

_____

_____

_____

101

19. What do the blind man's friends argue about when he comes back from the pool, having his sight? _____
_____

20. Right after you met Jesus, did people in your life see such a difference in you that they weren't sure it was really you? If so, please share your story. _____
_____
_____
_____
_____
_____
_____

21. What "I am" statement do you find in verse 9? Who said it and who is it about?
_____
_____

22. How closely does the blind man's testimony about his healing (see John 9:11) match the actual storyline of his healing (see John 9:6-7)? Did he embellish at all? _____

23. How can our personal testimony be similar to his? _____
_____
_____

CHAPTER 9

24. What did the blind man's testimony begin with? What was the initial focus of it? _____

25. What should be the main focus of our personal testimonies? _____
_____
_____

The blind man's testimony focused on Jesus. Ours should too.

In John 9:12 the blind man's neighbors ask where Jesus is and the blind man replies, "I don't know." Do you see the missed opportunity here? The neighbors may have wanted to go meet Jesus for themselves, and had the blind man known where Jesus was, he could have led them to Him.

26. Why is it so important for us to know where Jesus can be found?
_____
_____

27. Please read John 9:13-34. What were the Pharisees focused on primarily?
_____
_____

28. In John 9:24 the Pharisees tell the healed man what they know of Jesus. What was that? _____

29. Could they have been more wrong about who Jesus was? _____
_____

JUST JESUS

30. When the Pharisees give the healed man one more opportunity to give the glory to God rather than "this man they call Jesus." How does he respond?

___

31. When people try to pull you into an argument over the rules or laws of Christianity, do you defend the details or stick to what you know about what Jesus has done in your life? ___

___

32. Which of those approaches, defending details, or telling people what God has done for you personally, can they not argue with? ___

___

33. In John 9:27 we learn that the healed man has become one of Jesus' followers. How do we know that? ___

___

"Do you want to become his disciples too?"
—John 9:27

34. How did the Pharisees respond to his offer? ___

___

Again, John is showing us how spiritually blind the Pharisees were and how much insight a man who just met Jesus had.

35. In John 9:31-33 the healed man reminds the Pharisees of a few things. What are they? _____

_____

_____

_____

"If this man were not from God, he could do nothing."

—John 9:33

36. How do the Pharisees receive the healed man's teaching? _____

_____

_____

37. Comparing John 9:34 with John 9:2, how much had the Pharisees learned through this interaction? _____

_____

_____

38. Please read John 9:35-41. What did Jesus do when He heard the healed man had been thrown out by the Pharisees? _____

_____

_____

39. The wording in verses 39-41 can be confusing. Do your best to sum up what is being said here in your own words. _____

_____

_____

_____

_____

_____

_____

_____

John Chapter Ten

1. Spend some time listening to one of your favorite worship songs to get you focused on Jesus. Pray and ask God to teach you through His word as you study it. Ask Him to reveal hidden secrets and to open your eyes to what He wants you to learn in this time.

2. Please read John 10:1-42.

We risk missing what God has for us in Chapter 10 if we don't re-focus ourselves on where we were in Chapter 9. In the second half of Chapter 9, Jesus shows the Pharisees are spiritually blind, while a blind man is suddenly able to see, both literally and spiritually. Chapter 10 echoes the same contradiction of the spiritually blind versus those who have spiritual understanding, or sight.

Matthew Henry's Commentary on John 10 explains it this way, "The Pharisees supported themselves in their opposition to Christ with this principle, that they were the '*pastors of the church*,' and that Jesus, having no commission from them, was an intruder and an impostor, and therefore the people were bound in duty to stick to '*them*, against *him*.' In opposition to this, Christ here describes who were the false shepherds, and who the true, leaving them to infer what they were."[4]

3. With this in mind, please re-read John 10:1-22, then please list the characters in verses 1-5: _____

    _____

    _____

    _____

4. Verse 6 tells us that the Pharisees didn't understand Jesus' story in verses 1-5. Verse 7 tells us Jesus repeated and better explained His point to them. Please read John 10:7-13 then match the characters introduced to us in verses 1-5 with who we are told in these verses they represent:

- The man who does not enter the sheep pen by the gate, but climbs in by some other way – _____

- The man who enters by the gate – _____

- The gate – _____

- The watchman/shepherd – _____

- The sheep – _____

- A stranger – _____

- Hired hand – _____

5. Please summarize all you have learned in this exercise: _____

_____

_____

_____

_____

_____

_____

CHAPTER 10

6. If you could sum all of that up into one sentence, what would it be? _____

   _____

7. Focus now on the two additional "I ams" we meet in John 10:7-14. What does Jesus say He is? _____

   _____

   _____

"I am the gate; whoever enters through me will be saved."

—John 10:9

8. According to John 10:4, why do the sheep follow their shepherd?

   _____

"I am the good shepherd; I know my sheep and my sheep know me."

—John 10:14

9. Do you know what Our Shepherd's voice sounds like? When was the last time you heard Him speak to you, directly? _____

   _____

   _____

   _____

10. Why is it imperative that Jesus' voice is familiar to us? _____

    _____

    _____

John 10:5 tells us that sheep (believers) will never follow a stranger (someone other than Christ) because they don't recognize the stranger's voice. Think of a little girl and her mother in a department store. The two get separated and the mom calls out, "daughter" to which her daughter replies, "here I am". The daughter recognized her mom's voice. The other four kids nearby didn't reply to the mother's call because her voice wasn't familiar to them.

11. What additional information do we gain about the thieves or imposters in verse 10? _____

    _____

JUST JESUS

12. What do true spiritual leaders (and Jesus) do when they spot a wolf among their sheep? (see verse 11) _____

_____

_____

13. What do leaders who are not truly leading others to God through Christ do when they see a wolf among their sheep? (see verses 12-13) _____

_____

_____

14. According to John 10:17 and 18, would Jesus' life be taken from Him?

_____

_____

It's important to keep in mind that Jesus is prophesying about His future death on the cross. It hadn't happened yet, He was just foretelling it in parables and stories, so that after He had given His life, people would recall His stories and would believe that He was indeed the Son of God.

15. Please read John 10:22-30. What do the Jews ask Jesus to tell them plainly in verse 24? _____

16. How does Jesus respond to them? _____

_____

_____

_____

17. Please read John 10:28 carefully once more. What gift does Jesus give to His sheep? _____

110

CHAPTER 10

18. What was the last gift you were given? Did you DO anything to earn that gift, or was it just given to you because you are you? _____

_____

_____

19. According to Jesus, when will His sheep perish? _____

20. Who can snatch Jesus' sheep out of His hand? _____

21. According to these verses, once a person has accepted Jesus as their Lord and Savior, are they guaranteed a place in eternity or do they have to live a certain way or be actively following Christ in their everyday living for that to happen?

_____

_____

22. John 10:38 repeats a concept we learned in an earlier chapter of John. What, according to this verse, is a person to believe so they can "know and understand that the Father is in (Jesus) and (He) in the Father"? _____

_____

_____

"No one will snatch them out of my hand"
—Jesus

John Chapter Eleven

1. Spend some time listening to one of your favorite worship songs to get you focused on Jesus. Pray and ask God to teach you through His word as you study it. Ask Him to reveal hidden secrets and to open your eyes to what He wants you to learn in this time.

2. Please read John 11:1-57.

3. What are the first forty-four verses of John 11 about? _____
   _____

   Our author, John, just finished Chapter 10 with the idea that people should believe Jesus is the Son of God because of the miracles He performed, which they knew no ordinary man could do. Now, in Chapter 11, he shares with us what was one of Jesus' most meaning-filled miracles because it foreshadowed His own resurrection.

   According to Matthew Henry's commentary on John 11, Jesus' miracle of raising Lazarus from the dead is more often recorded than any other of Christ's miracles, not only because the miracle itself is great proof of Christ's mission, but because it was a sign of Christ's own resurrection, the crowning proof of who He was.[5]

4. What word did Martha and Mary send to Jesus in verse 3? _____
   _____

5. What was the reason for Lazarus' illness and subsequent death and resurrection? (see verse 4) _____
   _____

6. Please read verses 5-6 as if they were one complete sentence. What does this sentence convey about Jesus' timing? _____
   _____

   Jesus' explanation of His timing in John 11:9-10 can be confusing. What He is saying is that there is just enough time to do what has to be done (God's will) but that there is no time to waste.

7. How do you plan and spend your time? Mostly on God's will or your own? What can you do to change that if you're feeling called to? _____

_____

_____

_____

_____

8. In verse 8, Jesus doesn't even respond to the fear His disciples suggest He should have regarding returning to Judea. Why do you think that is? _____

_____

_____

_____

9. We see Jesus walking smack-dab in the center of His Father's will throughout the book of John. How do we know when we are walking in God's will in our own lives? _____

_____

_____

10. I love that Jesus' closest friends, His disciples, completely missed the point at times, probably because I do exactly what they did sometimes. Picture the scene in your head as you read verses 11-15.

11. Why, according to John 11:15, is Jesus glad He wasn't with Lazarus when he died? _____

    _____

    > "I am glad I was not there, so that you may believe."
    > —John 11:15

12. John 11:16 can be read in two totally different ways. How do you see the scene unfolding in two ways?

    Option 1: _____

    _____

    Option 2: _____

    _____

13. Please read John 11:17-37. What do you make of the second half of verse 20? Why do you think Mary stayed home? _____

    _____

    _____

14. What five evidences of Martha's faith do you see in verses 20-27?

    _____

    _____

    _____

    _____

JUST JESUS

> "I am the resurrection and the life. The one who believes in me will live, even though they die."
>
> —John 11:25

15. We can't skip over what might be the biggest "I AM" statement of them all. What does Jesus tell Martha He is in John 11:25? _____
    _____

16. What, in plain English, does Jesus mean in verses 25 and 26? _____
    _____
    _____
    _____
    _____

17. Reread John 11:25 and 26 once more, replacing the word, "her" in verse 25 with your name. For instance, I would read it this way, "Jesus said to Shelly, I am the resurrection and the life. He who believes in Me will live, even though he dies; and whoever lives and believes in Me will never die. Do you believe this?" How would you answer Jesus' question? _____
    _____
    _____

18. When Mary fell at Jesus' feet in John 11:32, how did Jesus receive her (see verses 33-35)? _____
    _____

19. Did Jesus ask Mary why she took so long to come to Him? Is there any evidence that He shamed her for not coming earlier with her sister? _____
    _____

Jesus is not a shamer. He is a healer.

CHAPTER 11

20. When you fall at Jesus' feet regarding something in your life, especially if it's something you feel He let you down about, do you accept Jesus' tear-filled reception of you or do you think He harbors disappointment in you for not coming to Him sooner? _____

_____

_____

_____

21. What question does Jesus ask in verse 34? _____

_____

22. Why would He have asked this question? Being God, He knew where Lazarus' body lay. _____

_____

23. What question do the people ask in verse 37? _____

_____

_____

_____

24. What is the irony of these two questions being asked together? _____

_____

_____

_____

_____

> "Take away the stone. Did I not tell you that if you believe, you will see the glory of God? Father, I thank you that you have heard me. I knew that you always hear me, but I said this for the benefit of the people standing here, that they may believe that you sent me. Lazarus come out! Take off the grave clothes and let him go."
>
> —Jesus

25. Please read John 11:38-44 in a unique way, reading only Jesus' words:

    We can look at Lazarus' death and resurrection as a foreshadowing of Christ's, but also as an analogy for our own spiritual life. Until we know Jesus, we are spiritually sick (as Lazarus was). Once we become Christ followers, we are called to "cast off our old way of life and anything that hinders us" (take away the stone that is keeping us in our dead way of life and remove our grave clothes which represent our old way of living) so that we can live in the freedom Christ died to give us.

26. Do you live in that freedom or are you still hiding in the cavern of your old life? Have you taken off the guilt and shame (your old grave clothes) of your past or are you still weighted down by them? _____

    _____

    _____

    _____

    _____

    _____

> Jesus died so we could live free from guilt and shame. Accept it. Celebrate it. You've been clothed in righteousness. Don't keep wearing your grave clothes. Think of it the way my teenage daughter would. If you had been given the most amazing, current, designer clothing to wear, would you instead keep wearing your old worn out, stained jeans? No way!!! Neither should we continue to wear our old selves when our freedom from them was bought for us at such a great price.

27. Please read John 11:45-53.

28. According to verse 45, what was the result of Jesus raising Lazarus from the dead? _____

> "Therefore many of the Jews who . . . had seen what Jesus did, believed in him."
>
> —John 11:45

29. Verse 46 tells us that not everyone who had seen Jesus raise Lazarus from the dead believed that Jesus was the Son of God. If you have not yet chosen to believe that Jesus is who He claimed to be, what type of miracle will it take to convince you? Would seeing Him raise someone from the dead be enough? What about seeing Him raise a ruined life up from the dead and into total freedom, would that do it? _____

_____

_____

_____

What sort of miracle is it going to take to convince you that Jesus really is who He says He is?

30. The chief priests and Pharisees knew what Jesus had been teaching. How do we know this, according to verses 47 and 48? _____

_____

_____

31. John 11:48 introduces us to the reason why the Jewish leaders wanted Jesus killed; because they were afraid He'd take their place, their jobs, and most importantly, their power. Often when a person is not interested in following Jesus it is because she doesn't want to have to give up her place, job, and most importantly, the power she believes she has over her own life. Before you met Jesus, did you think this way? _____

_____

_____

Many commentaries on John 11:48 suggest the fear that the chief priests and Pharisees exhibited was based on a complete misunderstanding of Jesus' motives because Jesus, in fact, had no political ambition whatsoever.[6]

32. How has your thinking changed since becoming a follower of Christ? _____

_____

_____

_____

33. Our next segment of scripture offers us comic relief. Please read John 11:49-50. What does Caiaphas say? _____

_____

_____

Caiaphas had no idea that he was actually prophesying as the high priest for that year. What he meant was, "it's better for us to kill Jesus and keep our places, jobs, roles and power (see vs 48) (to keep our nation) stable". What he unintentionally prophesied here was, "it is better that Jesus die to save mankind from our sins rather than to have mankind forever unable to be in relationship with God." Caiaphas thought killing Jesus would save his political position, but Jesus, giving up His life, did much more than that. His death and resurrection offered Caiaphas and anyone else who would choose to go there, forgiveness at the foot of the cross.

34. Please read John 11:54-57. Does this scene seem familiar to you? Do you remember studying similar scenes earlier in our study? Look back to John 6:15 and John 7:1 and 8. What do these verses have in common? _____

_____

_____

_____

35. What explanation does Jesus give for this in the last part of John 7:8? _____

    _____

36. How often do you rearrange your plans so that you can stay on God's timeline rather than push forward on your own? What do we risk when we live on our schedule rather than God's? _____

    _____

    _____

    _____

    _____

    _____

CHAPTER 11

"My time has not yet fully come."

—John 7:8

John Chapter Twelve

1. Spend some time listening to one of your favorite worship songs to get you focused on Jesus. Pray and ask God to teach you through His word as you study it. Ask Him to reveal hidden secrets and to open your eyes to what He wants you to learn in this time.

2. Please spend some more time learning about the Feast of Passover. www.jewsforjesus.org or www.chosenpeople.com are two great resources you might use.

3. Use the following website to get an understanding of the timeline of events of the Holy Week. www.understandchristianity.com/timelines/events-holy-week.

4. Please read John 12:1-50.

5. Now re-read John 12:1-3 envisioning the scene in your mind, then briefly describe the scene here. _____
   _____
   _____
   _____

6. Please read John 12:4-6. What happens in this scene? _____
   _____
   _____

Nard, the expensive perfume Mary poured on Jesus' feet, was typically used to prepare bodies for burial. In this instance, Mary unknowingly prepares Jesus' body for burial. The whole scene is one of Mary's humility since women didn't usually let down their hair in public and because tending to feet was a servant's job. We can hold this segment of scripture in contrast to the next one which is about a man lacking in humility.

7. What do we learn about Judas in verse 6? _____

_____

_____

8. From these two segments of scripture, what might we surmise about what Mary and Judas valued? _____

_____

9. When it comes to your own finances, are you more like Mary, willing to give freely to Jesus, or are you more like Judas? Why do you think that is?

_____

_____

_____

10. What insight do we get in verse 7 of Mary not being aware of God's will regarding using the perfume on this day? _____

_____

_____

_____

11. Share about a time you recently did something in God's will without even knowing you were. _____

_____

_____

_____

12. How does Jesus respond to Judas' shaming of Mary? (see verses 7 and 8)

   _____

   _____

13. While Jesus calls us to provide for the poor, His greater commandment is to put Him first, above all else. What does that look like, regarding God's will for our lives versus our own? _____

   _____

   _____

   _____

   _____

14. Please read John 12:9-11. Why were many Jews believing in Jesus according to these verses? _____

   _____

15. If you're using the NIV translation of the bible, what is the next section of scripture titled? _____

16. Please read John 12:12-19.

17. Why were there way more people than usual in Jerusalem at the time of Jesus' triumphal entry? _____

   _____

JUST JESUS

> "On the first day you are to take branches from ... palms ... and rejoice before the LORD your God for seven days."
>
> —Leviticus 23:40
>
> *Hosanna:*
> G5614 – oh save! And exclamation of adoration from the root word yasha H3467 which means to be free, to be safe, to free, avenge, deliver or rescue

18. Why, according to Leviticus 23:40, were they waving palm branches when Jesus came in to town? _____
_____
_____

19. Use your online study tool to find out the original word for "Hosanna" used in John 12:13. What does it mean and what does the root word from which it comes, mean? _____
_____
_____
_____
_____

20. Why is it significant that people were shouting this word as Jesus entered Jerusalem that day? _____
_____

According to Baker's Evangelical Dictionary of Biblical Theology, Hosanna is a "Joyful Aramaic exclamation of praise, apparently specific to the major Jewish religious festivals (especially Passover and Tabernacles) in which the Egyptian Hallel (Psalms 113-118) was recited. Originally an appeal for deliverance (Heb. hosia na, Please save Psalm 118:25), it came in liturgical usage to serve as an expression of joy and praise for deliverance granted or anticipated. When Jesus came to Jerusalem for His final presentation of himself to Israel, the expression came readily to the lips of the Passover crowds."[7]

21. Please read Psalms 118 out loud as if Jesus was saying it about Himself. Keep in mind these verses have been and are still read by Israelites when they celebrate the Jewish festivals that require pilgrimage, including Passover. As you read, look for words that foretell of Christ's death and resurrection and note them here:

_____

_____

_____

_____

"Give thanks to the Lord, for he is good; his love endures forever."

—Psalms 118:1

22. John 12:15 is repeating what was prophesied by Zechariah long ago. What does that prophecy say, according to Zechariah 9:9? _____

_____

_____

_____

23. What will our king have with Him according to this verse? (use the KJV translation) _____

24. Use your bible's notes on John 12:15 and/or Zechariah 9:9 to find out why Jesus rode in on a donkey, of all animals? _____

_____

_____

_____

JUST JESUS

25. John 12:16 tells us that even Jesus' disciples didn't understand what Jesus was saying at the time He said it. How do you think knowing these things helped them get through Jesus' trial and crucifixion? _____

_____

_____

_____

26. Why, according to verses 17-19, were many people going out to see Jesus?

_____

_____

27. Please read John 12:20-36. What is the significance of John telling us there were "some Greeks" worshiping at the Feast? _____

_____

_____

28. What did the Greeks want? _____

29. Many verses in John are about Jesus' "time". Please use your online study tool to search John Chapters 1-12 for instances where Jesus says His time has not yet come. Please note them here: _____

_____

_____

_____

_____

> Many people went out to meet Jesus because they had heard the testimony that He had raised Lazarus from the dead.

> "Sir, we would like to see Jesus."
> —John 12:21

CHAPTER 12

30. Is time coming or going, according to verse 23 and why is that significant?

    _____

    _____

    _____

31. Explain what the parable in John 12:24 and the subsequent lessons in verses 25
    and 26 mean to Christianity. _____

    _____

    _____

    _____

32. What mental struggle do we learn about in John 12:27-28? _____

    _____

    _____

    _____

33. It is not always easy for us to do God's will, and it wasn't always easy for Jesus to do
    it either. What might motivate us to follow God's will even when it's hard for us to
    do so? _____

    _____

    _____

    _____

34. What, according to verse 28, was Jesus' motive for going to the cross and rising
    again? _____

35. What did God say and who heard it in verses 28 and 29? _____

_____

_____

_____

36. Why do you think some people hear God when He speaks while others do not?

_____

_____

_____

37. In our current chapter, did everyone believe it was God speaking?

_____

_____

38. Jesus tells them in verse 30 that the voice they heard was for their benefit, not His. What do you think Jesus meant by this? _____

_____

_____

_____

_____

_____

CHAPTER 12

39. What three purposes did Jesus' crucifixion have, according to John 12:31 and 32? _____

_____

_____

_____

_____

_____

40. What was Jesus saying to the people in verse 35 when He was talking about the light? _____

_____

_____

41. Please read Luke 23:44 through the beginning of verse 45. What happened to the light, figuratively and non-figuratively, in these verses? How is this evidence of what Jesus was talking about in John 12:35? _____

_____

_____

_____

_____

_____

42. What plea does Jesus make to the people in John 12:36? _____

_____

_____

43. Please read John 12:37-43. What should have been enough to convince people to believe in Him, according to verse 37? _____

_____

44. Why were they not enough? _____

_____

_____

Are there any people in your life you feel have had plenty of opportunities to see God at work and believe in Him, but who haven't done so for some reason? If so, pray for God to remove the scales from their eyes so they can see, believe and live in His freedom.

45. We learn in John 12:42 that many even among the leaders did believe in Jesus but they would not profess their faith. Why wouldn't they? _____

_____

_____

_____

_____

CHAPTER 12

46. What was at the root of them not professing their faith? _____
_____
_____

47. Do you care more about what other people think about you or what God thinks about you? How is this evidenced in your life? _____
_____
_____
_____
_____

> Do you care more about what other people think about you or what God thinks about you? How is this evidenced in your life?

48. Please read John 12:44-50, then paraphrase verses 44-45. _____
_____
_____
_____
_____

49. Based on these two verses, is there any way to separate Jesus from God and vice versa? Can you get to God without going through Jesus? _____

50. Does Jesus judge people who hear His message but choose to not follow Him?
_____

JUST JESUS

When the sun shines, its goal is not to cast shadows, but it inevitably does. In the same way, Jesus, as the light, reveals our sin or our need for a savior just as the law, written down by Moses pointed out sin. Sometimes this revelation is taken as judgement, although it was never meant to be.

51. If Jesus doesn't judge them, why do we sometimes think we have a right to? _____
_____

52. Why doesn't Jesus judge those who have heard about Him, but have chosen not to believe in Him? _____
_____

53. In John 12:49 we learn that God had absolute control over Jesus' tongue. How do we know that? _____
_____
_____

54. Does God have control of your tongue in both what you say and how you say it? What would be proof of that being true in someone's life? _____
_____
_____
_____
_____
_____
_____

John Chapter Thirteen

1. Spend some time listening to one of your favorite worship songs to get you focused on Jesus. Pray and ask God to teach you through His word as you study it. Ask Him to reveal hidden secrets and to open your eyes to what He wants you to learn in this time.

Until this point the book of John has been mostly an account of Jesus' life, focusing on who He is and what He has done. Chapter 13 is a pivotal chapter where our author, John, shows Jesus handing the baton off to His disciples. Instead of Jesus doing the ministering, He now charges His disciples (and us) to "do as (He has) done".

2. Please read John 13:1-38.

3. Now let's narrow our focus onto John 13:1-17, probably a familiar story about Jesus washing His disciple's feet. Please re-read these verses now. Notice, once more, in the first verse, that Jesus' time had come. It was not fleeting.

4. In the second half of verse 1 we learn what the "full extent of Jesus' love" was. What was it literally and what was He pointing forward to? _____

    _____

    _____

    _____

    _____

5. What two things does our author point out that Jesus knew in verses 1-3?

_____

_____

_____

6. The word, "so" linking John 13:3 and 4 is important. It is the "why" behind Jesus' subsequent actions. In your own words explain why Jesus was able to humble Himself to wash His disciples' feet and to die on a cross. _____

_____

_____

_____

_____

_____

In verse 5 Jesus gives His disciples (and us) a lesson in humility and He demonstrates a principle of selfless service, both of which were about to be exemplified through the cross and both of which were to be continued by Jesus' followers.

7. Is there a story we studied in Chapter 12 that this scene reminds you of?

_____

_____

In Mary's act of humility, she was unknowingly preparing or anointing Jesus for His death and burial. In our current scene, Jesus is (very) knowingly preparing and anointing His disciples to share the gospel when He is no longer with them.

8. In John 13:7 Jesus says something He states repeatedly regarding what is happening now and what is going to come. What does He say?

_____

_____

Over and over again Jesus mentioned that although the people He was speaking to didn't understand what He was talking about when He was talking with them, they would eventually come to understand. Jesus did this so the people He foretold about events would look back, after Jesus' death and resurrection, and believe that Jesus was indeed the Son of God. They could believe not just because they had witnessed Him die and rise again, but because He had told them all about what was going to happen to Him before any of it occurred. This "extra level" of faith must have been helpful when people were coming up with all kinds of explanations for why Jesus' body was missing from His tomb.

9. In verse 8 Jesus tells Peter that unless He washes him, Peter can have no part in Jesus. What did Jesus mean, on a spiritual level? _____

_____

_____

_____

10. We find out Jesus knew something else in John 13:11. What else did He know?

_____

11. Jesus "knowing" things about His situation before they happened is similar to the blueprint for my life I often ask God for. However, because Jesus, while human, was also God, He knew what His future looked like. As Christ followers, we can have a similar "knowledge" of our lives by living in the spirit. Expand on this thought. _____

_____

_____

_____

_____

12. When was the last time you did a deliberate act of service for one of your brothers or sisters in Christ, and what was it? If you are having a hard time remembering one, what is something you could do as an act of service for someone this week? __

_____

_____

_____

13. Please read John 13:18-30.

14. Verse 19 is perhaps the clearest verse in this chapter. Here, Jesus vividly states WHY He is telling His disciples things now, before they happen. Why is He doing this? _____

_____

_____

In John 13:12-17 Jesus clearly explains the symbolism of His act of service (washing His disciple's feet). Jesus was a good leader; He did what He expected His followers to do and He didn't do what He didn't want His followers to do. In this scene, Jesus washes His disciples' feet as an act of humility, demonstrating what He expects His disciples to do for one another once He's gone. He is saying that He wants His followers (that's us) to perform deliberate acts of service for their brothers and sisters in Christ.

"I am telling you now before it happens, so that when it does happen you will believe that I am who I am."

—John 13:19

15. In a similar way to how Jesus told His disciples things before they happened, our author, John, prophecies about some things that are in our future in another book he wrote. Please read Revelation 1:1-3, then discuss how we are in a similar position to Jesus' disciples when He was telling them about things that were yet to come. Revisiting the paragraph in the sidebar on the previous page may be helpful. _

_____

_____

_____

_____

16. Throughout the book of John Jesus has often linked Himself to God. What did He say about this relationship in John 10:30? _____

_____

_____

17. In John 13:20 Jesus adds His disciples (that's us) to this equation. Please write the equation out below.

18. Thinking of missionaries or other people sent into the world by Jesus, what are we doing when we accept them into our hearts or homes? _____

_____

19. In the next verse, John 13:21, we learn that not all of Jesus' friends were good ones. What does this verse say about the state of Jesus' spirt because of that?

_____

JUST JESUS

20. Is it as comforting to you as it is to me that Jesus felt every emotion we've felt? Even, or maybe especially those stirred up in our relationships. If so, write a prayer thanking God for being your comfort in difficult times. _____

_____

_____

_____

_____

_____

Jesus felt every emotion you've felt. Let that comfort you.

21. Picture the scene in your mind from John 13:22-27, noting that the disciple mentioned in verse 23 is our author, John. It's not crystal clear, but I think our author leaned his ear back near Jesus' mouth when he asked Him who would betray Him and that our author, John, was probably the only disciple who knew it was Judas. How do you think this knowledge weighed on John? _____

_____

_____

_____

CHAPTER 13

22. What do Jesus' words to Judas, or Satan, in John 13:27 demonstrate about Jesus' understanding and commitment to His Father's plan? _____

_____

_____

_____

23. Please read John 13:31-35 then jot down the main points of this segment of scripture. _____

_____

_____

_____

_____

24. Please read John 13:36-38. We are shown another friendship problem in verses 37-38. How is Peter not encouraging his friend, Jesus, to follow His Father's plan?

_____

25. How do you think Jesus felt knowing yet another of his closest friends was going to betray Him and this time, it wasn't just once, but three times?

_____

> "A new command I give you: Love one another. As I have loved you, so you must love one another. By this everyone will know that you are my disciples, if you love one another."
>
> —John 13:34-35

26. Why do you think Jesus told Peter he would deny Him three times before the rooster crows? _____

_____

_____

_____

_____

_____

John Chapter Fourteen

1. Spend some time listening to one of your favorite worship songs to get you focused on Jesus. Pray and ask God to teach you through His word as you study it. Ask Him to reveal hidden secrets and to open your eyes to what He wants you to learn in this time.

2. Please re-read the short paragraph right before question #2 from our homework on Chapter 13.

   Through Chapters 1-12, which focus mostly on Jesus' life, our author uses some form of the word "love" twelve times.

   In Chapters 13-19, which focus primarily on Jesus instructions to His disciples of what they (we) should do and how they (we) should live, John uses a form of the word love thirty-five times.

   If we take an even closer look, we find he uses some form of the word love twenty-two times in Chapters 14-16, which are the main chapters where Jesus speaks directly to His disciples, teaching them how they should live when He is gone. This is significant because Jesus speaks the most about love when He is telling His disciples (that's us) how to live.

   He uses "love" ten times in the remaining two chapters (20-21).

3. What can we surmise, then, about what Jesus wanted His followers' lives to be marked by? _____

When an author really wants to make a point, he often uses repetition to get his idea across. For example, if he wants to accentuate his point in a certain place in his story that someone is really mad, he might use words related to being angry more times in that portion of his writing than he does elsewhere. It is important, therefore, for us to note where our author uses (some form of) the word "love".

John uses some form of the word "love" fifty-seven times in his testimony about Jesus' life.

The word love is also used in the other gospel accounts of Jesus' life. It is used thirteen times in Matthew, seven times in Mark and fifteen times in Luke.

4. Combined, the other gospel writers use "love" thirty-five times, which is nowhere near the fifty-seven times John uses it. Although each of the gospels is the good news of Jesus' love for mankind, which gospel do you think may be best to look to when we are sharing with someone how much Jesus loves them? _____
_____

5. Why our author uses love almost twice as much as the other gospel writers combined may be because he understood what it was like to be loved by Jesus. Please read the following verses and note what John is called in each verse.

- John 13:23 _____

- John 19:26 _____

- John 20:2 _____

- John 21:7 _____

- John 21:20 _____

6. What do these verses reveal to you about John's relationship with Jesus?
_____
_____
_____
_____

Do you understand that you are Jesus' beloved? In other words, do you know that Jesus dearly loves you?

CHAPTER 14

7. Keeping in mind that John wrote these words about himself, do you think he was being prideful when he mentioned (repeatedly) that Jesus loved him or do you think he just wanted us to understand that he knew he was loved by Jesus?

_____

_____

_____

_____

8. According to John 19:25-26, who was at the foot of the cross when Jesus was crucified? _____

_____

9. Just John. The only one of Jesus' disciples that stood by Him to the end was our author, John. Keeping question #5 in mind, what do you think it was that enabled John to stick with Jesus to the very end? _____

_____

_____

_____

Jesus calls His followers to love others, as He has loved them. Another way of saying this is that Jesus calls His followers to accept and receive His love for them SO THAT they can love others in a similar way. Until we realize the depth of Christ's love for us, we cannot fully love ourselves or others the way God wants us to.

JUST JESUS

Dear Jesus,

Please help me understand and accept the depth of Your love for me.

Amen

10. Do you understand and have you accepted to the core of your being that you are Jesus' beloved, that He loves you as much as He has ever loved anyone and that He desperately wants you to let those truths penetrate to the deepest parts of who you are? If not, take some time right now to write out a prayer to Jesus asking Him to help you accept the depth of His love for you. _____

_____

_____

_____

_____

_____

_____

11. As we move into Chapters 14-16 of the book of John, the chapters where John uses "love" more densely than anywhere else in his gospel, we are wise to take note of what Jesus chooses to talk about with His disciples. Using the headings in your NIV bible, please list what Jesus spends His breath on in each of these chapters.

Chapter 14 - _____

_____

_____

CHAPTER 14

Chapter 15 - _____

_____

_____

Chapter 16 - _____

_____

_____

12. Please read John 14:1-31.

13. At the end of Chapter 13 Jesus tells His disciples that He is going away and that they can't go with Him. With this in mind, how does Jesus open Chapter 14?

_____

_____

_____

"Do not let your hearts be troubled."
—John 14:1

14. What do you think Jesus meant in John 14:2 when He said there are many rooms in His Father's house? _____

_____

15. What does Jesus say at the end of verse 3 and through verse 4 to comfort His disciples about Him leaving them? _____

_____

"I will come back and take you to be with me that you also may be where I am."
—John 14:3

16. What, from our previous lessons, is "the way" to which Jesus refers in verse 4?

17. I love that some of Jesus' disciples were or at least behaved like complete nincompoops at times because it makes me feel better when I act like one. Jesus has just told His disciples that they know the way to the place He is going, but neither Thomas nor Phillip get it. How does Jesus respond to each of them?

18. What teachings is Phillip (and are we) reminded of in John 14:9-11? _____

19. In John 14:12-14 Jesus makes some astonishing promises. What does He say anyone who has faith in Him will be able to do? (vs 12) _____

"The person who trusts me will not only do what I'm doing but even greater things, because I, on my way to the Father, am giving you the same work to do that I've been doing."

—John 14:12
The Message

20. Why, according to John 14:13, will His followers be able to perform these miracles? _____

_____

21. What, according to verse 15 will Jesus' followers do if we love Him?

_____

Thinking through, or if you're an over-achiever, maybe skimming through our past chapters of John, what exactly were Jesus' commands and teachings? (We are not talking about the commandments of the Old Testament here, but rather, the directives Jesus gave to His disciples while He was with them in person.)

_____

_____

_____

_____

_____

_____

_____

_____

_____

JUST JESUS

22. If you had to sum up in ONE WORD, Jesus' teachings we've learned about so far in our study of the book of John, what would that word be? _____

23. What does Jesus promise God will give to us in John 14:16? _____
_____
_____

24. How long will that advocate or counselor be with us? _____

25. What is another name for this counselor, according to the beginning of John 14:17? _____

26. Where will this counselor live and be? (see verse 17) _____
_____
_____

As a follower of Jesus, you know the Spirit of Truth because he lives with you and he lives within you.

27. What teaching is Jesus reminding us of in the second part of John 14:19?
_____
_____
_____
_____

28. In verse 20 Jesus refers to a specific day. To what day is He referring? (You may need to use the notes in your bible to find out.) _____

CHAPTER 14

29. What will Jesus' disciples realize on resurrection day? _____

_____

_____

_____

_____

30. What do those who love Jesus do, according to John 14:21? _____

_____

_____

People who love Jesus keep His commands.

31. What were Jesus' commands, according to your most frequent answer in questions 18 and 19 of this chapter? _____

Judas' question in John 14:22 is hard to interpret. According to notes in my NIV bible, Judas is asking why Jesus is only around a little while and able to let only a limited number of people be eyewitnesses to His life rather than remaining with mankind forever on earth, so the whole world would have eyewitness accounts of who He was and what He did.

32. Jesus responds to Judas' question in verse 26 when He tells him again about the Holy Spirit who God will send. According to the second half of verse 26, what will the Holy Spirit do? _____

_____

33. In verse 27, what does Jesus leave with and give to His disciples?

_____

The Holy Spirit teaches us and reminds us of what Jesus has said to us.
—John 14:26

> "Do not let your hearts be troubled and do not be afraid."
> —John 14:27

34. What, according to the end of verse 27 will that peace accomplish in them?

   _____

   _____

35. In John 14:29 Jesus tells His disciples again that He's telling them about things before they happen. Why is He doing this? _____

   _____

36. In verse 30 we learn that someone is coming. What does the verse call Him and who is it? _____

37. Does Satan have any hold over Jesus? (see verse 30) _____

38. How and why might Jesus' death on the cross have appeared to onlookers as if Satan had won? _____

   _____

   _____

   _____

39. If Satan had no hold over Jesus, why did Jesus' death make it look like he did? (see verse 31) _____

   _____

   _____

   _____

CHAPTER 14

40. In the same way that Jesus' love for His Father allowed Him to be obedient to the point of death on the cross, our love for Jesus must lead us to be obedient to live according to His teachings. What, once more, were His primary teachings up to this point? _____

_____

_____

_____

_____

_____

_____

Jesus followers love Him and they believe Him so they obey Him.

41. The very end of John 14:31 tells us Jesus and His disciples left. Where do you think they went? _____

_____

John Chapter Fifteen

CHAPTER 15

1. Spend some time listening to one of your favorite worship songs to get you focused on Jesus. Pray and ask God to teach you through His word as you study it. Ask Him to reveal hidden secrets and to open your eyes to what He wants you to learn in this time.

2. Please read through John 15:1-27.

3. What "I am" does Jesus add to His resumé in verses 1 and 5?
   _____

   Please research online to learn about pruning grapevines.

   > Use Google to learn how, why and when to prune grapevines.

4. In gardening, what is the purpose of a branch and what is the purpose of the vine? _____
   _____
   _____

5. After reading a bit about pruning grapes, which branches (on a grape vine) bear fruit? _____
   _____
   _____

6. Please re-read John 15:1-8, then label who the parts of the vine represent for each character in the scene.

- The True Vine – _____

- The Gardener – _____

- A branch that bears no fruit – _____

- A branch that bears fruit – _____

7. What does God do to every branch that doesn't bear fruit? What does He do to every branch that does bear fruit? (see vs 2) _____
_____
_____

8. Use your online study tool to look up the original word and its meaning of the word translated, "remain" in John 15:4. _____
_____
_____

9. How would you define abiding in Jesus? _____
_____
_____
_____

CHAPTER 15

10. Do you abide in Jesus as much as you would like? If not, what do you think keeps you from abiding in Him? What can you do to begin to abide in Him today? _

_____

_____

_____

11. According to verse 4, what can a branch *not* do by itself?

_____

12. Can we, as Christ followers, "bear fruit" if we are not abiding in Christ?

_____

13. According to John 15:5, what can we do if we remain in Christ and what can we do apart from Him? _____

_____

14. What two things does bearing much fruit bring about? (see verse 8)

_____

_____

15. If you had to summarize John 15:1-8 into one WORD, what would it be?

_____

16. Please read John 15:9-17. We are told to remain in something in verse 9. What is that? _____

17. Verse 10 tells us how to remain in Christ's love. How do we do that? _____

_____

"If you remain in me and I in you, you will bear much fruit; apart from me you can do nothing."
—John 15:5

Abide:
to continue to be present with

"If you keep my commands, you will remain in my love."
—John 15:10

157

JUST JESUS

18. Does that mean that Jesus doesn't love us if we aren't being obedient?

   _____

   _____

19. How do we know that? Please read Romans 5:6-8 to answer this question.

   _____

   _____

"While we were still sinners, Christ died for us."
—Romans 5:8

20. Why does Jesus want us to obey His commands? (see John 15:11) _____

   _____

   _____

21. What, then, is the result of us remaining in Christ's love and being obedient to Him? _____

   _____

22. What, according to verse 12, does Jesus command us to do? _____

   _____

"Love each other as I have loved you"
—John 15:12

23. How has Jesus loved us? _____

   _____

24. With that in mind, how are we supposed to love each other? _____

   _____

CHAPTER 15

25. Jesus defines how He has loved us another way in John 15:13. What does it say? _____

_____

26. What does it look like for us to 'lay down our lives', figuratively, for one another? _____

_____

_____

27. How can we tell if we are Jesus' friends, according to verse 14? _____

_____

28. What did He command us to do? (see verse 12) _____

_____

29. When friends are made, usually a pair of people decide to befriend one another. Our friendship with Jesus is a little different than this. Why, according to John 15:16? _____

_____

_____

30. Why did He choose us to be His friends? _____

_____

_____

"Greater love has no one than this: to lay down one's life for one's friends."
—John 15:13

JUST JESUS

31. What will the Father give us if we do what we're told to do (bear fruit) in verse 16? _____

This doesn't mean we can ask God for a Porsche, in Jesus' name, and He'll give it to us. It means that IF we are living in God's will and are asking for things in God's will, He will give them to us. God put us here on mission and He will give us anything we ask for to help us accomplish that mission.

32. What command does Jesus remind us of in John 15:17? _____

_____

Jesus doesn't suggest or ask us to love each other. He commands us to.

33. How are you personally doing with this commandment? Are you loving others the way Jesus loves you? If so, share some stories of how you've demonstrated your love to others in the past month or so. If not, ask the Lord for forgiveness and for Him to help you love others the way He loves you. _____

_____

_____

_____

_____

_____

34. If you had to summarize John 15:9-17 into one WORD, what would it be?

_____

35. Please read John 15:18-27.

CHAPTER 15

36. Jesus has just finished our earlier segment of scripture with the command to "love each other". Now He opens this section with an opposite emotion. What emotion is it and who has it toward whom? _____
_____

37. Why does the world hate Jesus followers? (see verse 19) _____
_____
_____

"You do not belong to the world . . . . That is why the world hates you."
—John 15:19

38. Let's look at John 15:21 for a minute. Why will the world persecute Jesus' followers? _____
_____

39. Have you witnessed this in your own life, where people are okay with you talking about God, but as soon as you bring up Jesus' name they get offended? If so, share an example or two. _____
_____
_____
_____
_____

40. Why is this, according to John 15:21b? _____
_____

JUST JESUS

41. In John 15:22 Jesus tells us why some people are guilty of sin. Why is it?

   _____

   _____

   _____

42. What can we infer from this verse about the guilt of people who have NEVER heard the gospel message? Will that sin be held against them? _____

43. John 15:25 ends with a poignant statement. What does Jesus say here?

   _____

44. Have you ever felt hated by the world for no reason? Do you now have a clearer understanding of why the world may sometimes hate you for no reason?

   _____

   _____

45. What is the real reason believers are sometimes unfairly hated? _____

   _____

   _____

46. Unfortunately, throughout history Christians have sometimes been hated for very good reasons. List some of the most embarrassing here. _____

   _____

   _____

   _____

CHAPTER 15

47. John 15:26 in the NIV calls the Holy Spirit our "Advocate". Look at multiple other translations, and list what the Advocate is called in those places.

___

___

___

___

> The Holy Spirit is our Advocate, our Comforter, our Helper, our Counselor, our Friend and the Spirit of Truth.

48. What other name does He call Him later in the same verse?

___

49. What will the Holy Spirit do when He goes out from the Father?

___

50. What do you think the Holy Spirit's testimony about Jesus is like and who do you think it's to? ___

___

___

51. Given the Holy Spirit's example, is it okay for our testimony about Jesus to be negative, shaming, condemning, or boring? ___

52. Again, keeping the example of the Holy Spirit's testimony in mind, should we testify about Jesus to anyone and everyone, or mainly to those who have demonstrated they are willing to listen? ___

___

___

JUST JESUS

Abide!

Love!

Testify!

It is interesting to note the progression in John 15. In the beginning of the chapter, Jesus' followers are called to abide in Christ. When we abide in Christ, we are able to do what we are called to do, which is what the middle portion of John 15 is about, loving one another. Our love for each other then leads us to testify about Jesus to others, which is what we are called to do in the last section of John 15. In other words, when we abide in Christ, we are able to truly love one another and when we love one another, we will inevitably share our testimony of Christ with others.

53. What does Jesus mean in John 15:27 when He says that His disciples must also testify about Him since they've been with Him from the beginning? _____

_____

_____

54. If you had to summarize John 15:18-27 into one WORD, what would it be?

_____

55. Do you regularly share your story of what Jesus has done in your life with others? Do you frequently testify to His goodness in your life? If not, what can you do to make testifying about Jesus a regular part of your day? _____

_____

_____

56. Please revisit earlier questions #15, 34 and 54, and list the words you chose here:

- John 15:1-8 _____

- John 15:9-17 _____

- John 15:18-27 _____

57. What are we hoping for when we introduce others to Jesus? _____

_____

_____

John Chapter Sixteen

1. Spend some time listening to one of your favorite worship songs to get you focused on Jesus. Pray and ask God to teach you through His word as you study it. Ask Him to reveal hidden secrets and to open your eyes to what He wants you to learn in this time.

2. Please read through John 16:1-33.

3. What are the words, "all this" in verse 1 referring to? (your bible may have a note for this phrase). _____
   _____
   _____

4. What is Jesus telling His disciples in verses 2-3? _____
   _____
   _____

5. John 16:4 tells us why Jesus is telling His disciples these unsettling things. Why did He? _____
   _____
   _____

6. What do verses 5 and 6 say? _____
   _____
   _____

> "I have told you this, so that when their time comes you will remember that I warned you about them."
>
> —John 16:4

7. Why is it better for the disciples for Jesus to go away and who or what will He send them when He's gone? (see verse 7) _____
_____
_____

8. John 16:8-11 are about what the Holy Spirit will convict the world of. Please read those verses now. Then describe how the Holy Spirit will convict the world in regard to:

- Sin – _____
_____
_____

- Righteousness – _____
_____
_____

- Judgment – _____
_____
_____

9. John 16:12-15 tell us more about what the Holy Spirit does for us. What else does He do? _____
_____
_____

The Holy Spirit guides Jesus followers into the truth. He tells us what is to come and He glorifies Jesus by telling us what Jesus told Him.

CHAPTER 16

10. Please read John 16:16-19. What did the disciples not understand?

    _____

    _____

11. What do you think these verses mean? _____

    _____

    _____

    _____

    _____

12. In verses 20-22 Jesus uses a worldly example to get a point across to His disciples. What example does He use and what is the point He is trying to make?

    _____

    _____

    _____

    _____

    _____

> "No one will take away your joy."
> —John 16:22

13. What does Jesus mean in verse 22 when He says, "no one will take away your joy"? _____

    _____

    _____

14. In John 16:23-24 Jesus explains that the way His disciples communicate with God is going to change. How? _____

    _____

JUST JESUS
Because of Jesus' death and resurrection, His followers have direct access to God. No middle man is needed.

15. Jesus further explains this in verse 26. What does He tell the disciples there?

_____

_____

_____

In John 16:25 Jesus admits to His disciples that He's often spoken figuratively but He promises that a time will come when He will tell them plainly about His Father. Then, He only makes them wait two sentences until He implements His plain speech and says, "I came from the Father and I'm going back to the Father." It doesn't get much clearer than that.

16. Verse 27 tells the disciples (and us) why they are able to have direct contact with God. Why is that? _____

_____

_____

17. How do Jesus' disciples respond to His plain language? (see verse 29)

_____

_____

18. How does Jesus respond to them in verse 31? _____

_____

"Do you now believe?"
—John 16:31

19. While Jesus may seem celebratory in verse 31, He warns His disciples in verse 32. What does He warn them about? _____

_____

20. Jesus is referring to everything He's said in John 16:17-22 when in verse 33 He says, "I have told you these things". Why, according to verse 33, did Jesus tell His disciples all this stuff? _____

21. What does Jesus reiterate to His disciples (and us) in the second part of John 16:33? _____

CHAPTER 16

22. What hope does Jesus give His disciples and us in the last part of verse 33?

   _____

   _____

   _____

23. John 16:33 can be summarized in three statements. Write them here:

   In Jesus we … _____

   In the world we … _____

   We can celebrate though, because Jesus has … _____

24. What does it mean to you that Jesus has "overcome the world"? _____

   _____

   _____

   _____

   _____

25. Based on what we've learned so far in our study of the Book of John, please fill in the blanks:

   1. Jesus is the _____ of _____.

   2. We must _____ belief or unbelief.

   3. The ____ _____ (who would be sent to us) will draw us to Christ and help us experience a relationship with Jesus and God

> "I have told you these things, so that in me you may have peace. In this world you will have trouble. But take heart! I have overcome the world."
>
> —John 16:33

4. John 16:33 introduces a new idea; daily _____ _____ and a resurrection into eternity with God is ours for the taking because of what Jesus did for us on the cross.

John Chapter Seventeen

1. Spend some time listening to one of your favorite worship songs to get you focused on Jesus. Pray and ask God to teach you through His word as you study it. Ask Him to reveal hidden secrets and to open your eyes to what He wants you to learn in this time.

2. If your bible has section headings for John Chapter 17, please write them here:

   _____

   _____

   _____

3. John 17, Jesus' longest recorded prayer in scripture begins with Jesus addressing His "Father". A quick word study reveals that the same word translated, "Father" here (G3962) is used 419 times throughout the bible. 115 of those times is in our book of John. More than a quarter of the times the word Father is used in scripture is in the book of John. Why do you think that is? _____

   _____

   _____

   _____

   _____

   _____

Of the 419 times the word "Father" is used in scripture, 115 are in the book of John.

4. What does the fact that Jesus started His prayer with a familiar word of endearment rather than a word of respect or honor mean to you? _____

_____

_____

5. If you have an NIV Study Bible, please use the Life of Christ timeline you'll find in the book of John to determine where we are in Jesus' life as we begin Chapter 17. If you don't have an NIV Study Bible, flip back through the section headings for John 16 in your bible to get the same information. What was Jesus doing just before He began praying? _____

_____

_____

6. What happens shortly after Jesus prays? (the section heading for Chapter 18 might be helpful). _____

7. Now that we know where we are in Jesus' life, please read through John 17:1-26. Next please re-read verses 1-5, noting this is Jesus' prayer for Himself.

8. In verse 1 we learn that, "the time has come". Please note what the following verses say about this time.

Matthew 26:18 _____

Mark 14:35 _____

Mark 14:41 _____

John 7:6 _____

John 7:8 _____

John 7:30 _____

John 8:20 _____

John 12:23 _____

John 13:1 _____

9. What, exactly, is this time referring to? _____
_____

10. Is there any doubt in your mind that God was in control over every aspect of Jesus' life, even the seemingly horrible events of the Passion Week?
_____

11. Do you ever doubt that God is in control of every aspect of your life, even the difficult things? Do you ever doubt He is in control of every aspect of your kids' or your families' lives? Why do you think that is? _____
_____
_____
_____
_____

JUST JESUS

12. What kind of relationship must Jesus have had with His Father to be able to tell people so many times that His time had not yet come? _____

_____

_____

13. In John 17:3 Jesus clearly states what eternal life is. What does He say and why do you think He prayed it, since God would've already known what it was?

_____

_____

_____

> "Now this is eternal life: that they know you, the only true God, and Jesus Christ, whom you have sent."
> —John 17:3

14. How did Jesus bring God glory according to John 17:4? _____

_____

> "I have brought you glory on earth by finishing the work you gave me to do."
> —John 17:4

15. How might we bring God glory in our lives? _____

_____

16. How can we know what that work is? _____

_____

_____

Jesus' words in John 17:5 are a request to His Father to return Him to His previous position of glory. Before Jesus came to earth He was one with God. At this point, Jesus is asking His dad to restore Him to His original place of honor and authority.

17. Please read John 17:6-10, noting Jesus is now praying for His disciples.

CHAPTER 17

18. What does Jesus say He has done for His disciples, "those whom you gave Me out of the world" in verse 6? _____

19. How did Jesus reveal God to them, according to verse 8? _____
_____

20. What three important actions in someone getting to know Jesus are demonstrated in this verse? _____
_____
_____
_____
_____

21. Has someone revealed God to you and if so, how did they do it? _____
_____
_____
_____
_____

22. Have you made the conscious decision to believe the gospel message, that God sent Jesus, His only son, to earth to live and die in order to give us access to God and that by believing in Jesus' life, death and resurrection, we can be freed from our sin and live in an intimate relationship with Jesus and God for all eternity? _____
_____

23. If not, what is keeping you from making that decision? _____

_____

_____

_____

_____

24. John 17:9 makes me smile. What special privilege do followers of Christ have according to this verse? _____

_____

_____

25. Please read John 17:11-12 pretending you are eavesdropping on Jesus' prayer time about His disciples. What predicament is Jesus praying about here?

_____

_____

_____

26. What does Jesus ask His Father to do, specifically, in verse 11? _____

_____

27. Why did Jesus want God to protect His disciples? For what purpose did He ask for them to be protected? (see verse 11) _____

_____

_____

28. Please read John 17:13-19, the remainder of Jesus' prayer for His disciples.

    Jesus' statement, "I am coming to you now", in verse 13 reminds us that His life was not taken and He was not unwillingly killed. Rather, He voluntarily died for us so we might have relationship with His Father.

    Later in verse 13, Jesus explains that He is saying these things so His disciples might, "have the full measure of (His) joy within them". Jesus is saying that the only way to experience full joy is to live in an intimate relationship with Him, the Christ, who is the source of all joy.

29. Do you find it odd that Jesus is talking about His joy considering where He is in His life (after preparing His disciples for His departure and right before being arrested)? _____

    _____

    _____

    _____

    _____

30. What does Jesus' followers having His word (the bible) have to do with the world hating them (see verse 14) _____

    _____

    _____

> "They are not of the world."
> —Jesus

CHAPTER 17

JUST JESUS

G2889; kosmos is used fifteen times in the other three gospel accounts combined. It is used fifty-seven times in John.

31. What phrase does Jesus say about His disciples that is repeated in John 17:14 and 16? _____

32. Use your online tool to find out how many times the word translated as "world" is used in each of the other gospel accounts and note them here:

    • Matthew – _____

    • Mark – _____

    • Luke – _____

33. Now find out how many times the word translated as "world" is used in our book of John and note that here: _____

34. Our author, John, (and Jesus) is using repetition again to make another important point. Why do you think they use the word "world" so many times while Jesus is praying for His disciples? It is used seventeen times in our current chapter, John 17 alone. _____
_____
_____

"My prayer is not that you take them out of the world but that you protect them from the evil one."

—John 17:15

35. What does Jesus specifically ask His Father for in John 17:15? _____
_____

36. Would you say that one of Jesus' biggest concerns is for His disciples to be protected as they live in, but not of, the evil world? _____

37. Please fill in the number of verses in each section of Jesus' prayer:

    • Jesus' prayer for Himself (vs 1-5) – ____ verses

- Jesus' prayer for His disciples (vs 6-19) – ____ verses

- Jesus' prayer for all believers (vs 20-26) – ____ verses

38. Do the number of verses in each section of Jesus' prayer support your answer to question #36? _____

39. In John 17:17 Jesus asks His Father to "sanctify" His disciples by the truth, which is His Word. Please use your online tool to find out what the word translated as "sanctify" was originally and what it means. _____

_____

_____

_____

_____

40. What is Jesus asking God to do to His disciples, then? _____

_____

_____

_____

41. What effect does daily application of God's word have on a person?

_____

_____

_____

JUST JESUS

42. In John 17:18 Jesus equates His sending His disciples into the world with God's sending Jesus into the world. What does that mean for us as followers of Christ? _____
_____
_____

43. In verse 19, who does Jesus sanctify Himself for? _____

44. Why does Jesus sanctify Himself? _____
_____

45. Do you hear a "secret message" in Jesus' prayer to His Father in verse 19? Think about what Jesus is about to do (lay down His life) and how that act of dedicating Himself to God and to God's plan for humanity is sanctification. Discuss.
_____
_____
_____

46. Please read John 17:20-23, the beginning of Jesus' prayer for all believers.

47. In verse 20 Jesus tells us another group of people He is praying for. Who is He talking about? _____
_____

48. Have you heard the disciples' message about Jesus? (You are doing a bible study on it this moment, so your answer should be an emphatic, "Yes!") Have you chosen to believe in Jesus because of that message and if so, do you understand that Jesus was praying for you in this John 17 prayer? _____

How does it make you feel to know that right before He went to the cross, Jesus prayed for you?

CHAPTER 17

49. How does it make you feel, knowing that right before Jesus was going to die, He prayed for you, someone who wouldn't even live for a couple thousand years after His death and resurrection? _____

_____

_____

50. If you had to use one word to summarize what John 17:21-23 is about, what word would you use? _____

51. Why, according to the latter part of verse 23, did Jesus want His believers to "be brought to complete unity"? _____

_____

52. As believers in Christ, why is it important for us to live in unity with one another? _____

_____

_____

53. What do we risk if we are not unified? _____

_____

_____

54. Please read John 17:24-26. What does Jesus ask His Father for in verse 24?

_____

_____

Unity:
the state of being; oneness; a whole or totality as combining all its parts into one; the state or fact of being united or combined into one, as of the parts of a whole; unification; absence of diversity, unvaried or uniform character; oneness of mind, feeling, etc., as among a number of persons, concord, harmony, or agreement. In Mathematics: the number one, a quantity regarded as one, identity. In literature and art: a relation of all the parts or elements of a work constituting a harmonious whole and producing a single general effect.[8]

JUST JESUS

55. What does Jesus tell His Father in verses 25 and 26? _____

_____

_____

56. Why, according to verse 26, will Jesus continue to make God known to mankind? _____

_____

57. Looking over your study for today, what was John 17 all about? _____

_____

_____

John 17 is a record of Jesus' prayers for Himself, for His disciples, and for all believers.

John Chapter Eighteen

1. Spend some time listening to one of your favorite worship songs to get you focused on Jesus. Pray and ask God to teach you through His word as you study it. Ask Him to reveal hidden secrets and to open your eyes to what He wants you to learn in this time.

2. Please read John 18:1-40, then focus more closely by re-reading verses 1-3.

3. According to verse 1, what had Jesus just finished doing before this scene takes place? _____

4. Who met Jesus and His disciples in the olive grove? _____
   _____
   _____

5. What were they carrying? _____

6. Based on what they were carrying, what time of day must it have been?
   _____

7. Because they were carrying weapons, what state of mind must the soldiers have been in? Does it seem like they were anticipating resistance from Jesus? If so, why do you think that was? _____
   _____
   _____

8. Please read John 18:4-9.

JUST JESUS

zeteo; G2212
to seek in order to find; to seek a thing; to seek [in order to find out] by thinking, meditating, reasoning, to enquire into; to seek after, seek for, aim at, strive after

9. Use your online study tool to find out what the original word for the word translated "want" in verse 4 is. What is the original word and what does it mean? _____

_____

_____

_____

_____

10. Please look up Matthew 6:33, 7:7 and 8. What word is used in all three of these verses? _____

11. What is Jesus telling them to seek in each of those verses?

- Matthew 6:33 – _____

- Matthew 7:7 – _____

- Matthew 7:8 – _____

When Jesus uses the same word with the Roman soldiers (in John 18) as He did in these other accounts, He is using a play on words. While on the surface, it seems like He is asking the soldiers, "Who are you looking for?", in reality He is asking them a much deeper, spiritual question, "What are you seeking after in your life?"

CHAPTER 18

12. If a friend asked you the same question, "What are you seeking after in your life?", how would you answer? _____

_____

_____

_____

What are you seeking after in your life?

13. If Jesus asked you the same spiritual question, how would you answer Him?

_____

_____

_____

_____

14. John 18:4-9 is a conversation between Jesus and the Roman soldiers. How does Jesus respond when the soldiers tell Him they are looking for Jesus of Nazareth? (see verse 5) _____

15. Why do you think Jesus told the soldiers to let His disciples go, since the soldiers were looking for Him? _____

16. Please read John 18:10-11, picturing the scene in your head. What happens here? _____

_____

_____

JUST JESUS

The word "Malchus" means "king or kingdom". When Jesus scolded Peter He was in effect telling him to put away his sword and allow God's "Kingdom" plan to unfold. If Peter had gotten his way, Jesus would not have gone to the cross and God's Kingdom plan of redemption could have been impeded.

17. How does Jesus respond to Peter's efforts to "help" Him? _____
_____
_____
_____

18. Who was Malchus, according to verse 10? _____

19. How is this title similar to, but lesser than Jesus' title? _____
_____
_____

20. The interaction in John 18:10-11 is recorded in the book of Luke as well. Please read Luke 22:47-51, then note what additional information Luke gives us about what Jesus does to the man's ear. _____
_____

Jesus, "touched the man's ear and healed him."
—Luke 22:51

21. When I read John 18:12-14 I feel like I missed something. "Then . . . (they) arrested Jesus". Why? If they arrested anyone it should've been Peter for cutting off a guy's ear. What right did they have to arrest Jesus? _____

22. What, according to the end of verse 12, did the soldiers do to Jesus?
_____

23. Had Jesus demonstrated any need to be bound by them? Had He ever tried to get away or acted like He was unwilling to go with them? _____
_____

CHAPTER 18

24. We met Caiaphas before in Chapter 11, where he was inadvertently prophesying. John 18:14 reminds us what his prophecy was about. What was it?

   _____

   _____

   _____

   _____

25. Please read John 18:15-18 and 25-27. What happens in these verses?

   _____

26. Why is it significant that Peter denies knowing Christ three times?

   Jesus: *"I AM"*
   Peter: *"I am not"*

   _____

   _____

   _____

   _____

27. How does Peter respond the first two times he is confronted about being one of Jesus' disciples? _____

28. How do Peter's responses differ from the "I ams" we've heard from Jesus?

   _____

   _____

29. Please read John 18:19-24 and picture the scene in your mind.

In John 18:20-21 I'm not sure if Jesus is taunting Annas or if Jesus is simply reminding him that a lot of people have heard about Jesus, His miracles and His teachings. Remember, the reason the priests and Pharisees wanted Jesus dead was because they feared they would lose their positions of authority and power if people continued to join Jesus' movement.

30. Please revisit question #23 in this week's homework, then read John 18:20-21 once more. What words in these verses also show that Jesus wasn't hiding or doing anything in secret, but that He was open and willing to walk the path to the cross? _____

_____

_____

_____

31. What does the last part of John 18:21 say? _____

_____

32. Do you hear the threat in Jesus' voice in this statement? It's almost as if He is saying, "you might silence me, but you're not going to silence everyone about me". _____

_____

33. In verse 22 Jesus is struck in the face by one of the officials. Do you think this is because the official heard Jesus' warning in His previous statement?

_____

_____

CHAPTER 18

34. Two parallel stories are taking place in these beginning verses of John 18. Please re-read verse 10 and verse 22, then explain how they are similar.

_____

_____

_____

_____

35. What words in John 18:24 infer that the soldiers, Annas and the chief priests' officials were afraid of Jesus? _____

36. Where was Jesus sent next? (see verse 24) _____

37. What does John, our author, tell us about the time Jesus was before Caiaphas?

_____

38. Please read Matthew 26:57-68 to learn about Jesus' time before Caiaphas.

39. According to Matthew 26:59, what were the chief priests and the Sanhedrin looking for? _____

_____

40. Why were they looking for this evidence? _____

_____

41. How much evidence did they find, according to Matthew 26:60?

_____

They had Jesus bound.

42. What two "charges" were made against Jesus:

    - in Matthew 26:61 – _____

    _____

    - in Matthew 26:63 and 64 – _____

    _____

43. How did the chief priest respond in Matthew 26:65? _____

    _____

44. Use your online study tool to look up what both instances of the word translated, "blasphemy" in Matthew 26:65 mean, in their original form, then write them here:

    First occurrence in vs 65: _____

    _____

    _____

    Second occurrence in vs 65: _____

    _____

    _____

45. What did the Sanhedrin decide Jesus was worthy of, according to Matthew 26:66? _____

CHAPTER 18

46. The NIV study bible has a note next to the word translated, "death" in verse 66. If you follow the note, it leads us to Leviticus 24:16. What does that verse teach us about what the penalty for blasphemy was according to Jewish law?

_____

_____

_____

The penalty for blaspheming the name of the Lord was stoning.

47. Does it make any sense, considering this law, that they would crucify Jesus rather than stone Him? _____

48. Why is it ironic that Jesus would be charged with the crime of blasphemy?

_____

_____

_____

_____

49. What did the Sanhedrin do to Jesus next? (see Matthew 26:67 and 68)

_____

_____

50. When I picture this scene in my mind, I can hardly look at Jesus. The Son of God is having His face spat upon. Yet, there have been times in my life when I have figuratively done the same thing to Him. Have you ever (figuratively) spat upon Jesus' face? _____

Have you ever "spat" upon Jesus' face?

JUST JESUS

51. How does it make you feel to know that Jesus' reason for dying on His cross was so that we could each be forgiven for the times we "spit in His face", when we choose to sin rather than follow Him? _____
_____
_____
_____

52. We've been away from our book of John for quite a while. Please return to it and read John 18:28-40.

53. Where, according to John 18:28, was Jesus taken next? _____
_____

> The Jews did not enter Pilate's palace because they did not want to become unclean by going into a gentile's home. If they had, they would've had to spend a few days purifying themselves, and they would have then missed the Passover Feast.

54. How are the Jews being hypocritical by not wanting to enter a gentile's home, yet leading Jesus through trials with false accusations? _____
_____
_____
_____

55. What does Pilate, the Roman governor, ask the Jews in John 18:29?
_____

> "What charges are you bringing against this man?"
> —John 18:29

56. How do the Jews respond? _____
_____
_____

57. From Pilate's response in verse 31, we can see he is wise. How do we know this?

_____

_____

_____

58. John 18:31 tells us the Jews objected to taking Jesus back to their own courts. Verse 32 tells us why. Why was that? _____

_____

_____

59. Please read Matthew 20:18 and 19. What had Jesus said would happen to Him?

_____

_____

_____

> "This took place to fulfill what Jesus had said about the kind of death he was going to die."
> —John 18:32

You may be getting tired of flipping back and forth from our book of John to Matthew's account of Jesus' life in his book, but it's important to remember that both Matthew and John were eye-witnesses of Jesus' life. John saw and heard some things Matthew did not, and vice versa. In this case, it seems Matthew had heard Jesus prophecy about His trial and death, while John may not have been privy to that information. All the more reason to be amazed by the consistency of scripture. What one apostle and author has documented as prophecy another has written as historical fact. God's Word, just like God Himself, is amazingly consistent. If you have an NIV Study Bible you can dig into this idea further by looking through "The NIV Harmony of the Gospels". It's located at the end of the book of John in my NIV Study Bible. If your bible doesn't have it, search for something similar online.

JUST JESUS

"The reason I was born and came into the world is to testify to the truth."

—John 18:37

60. In John 18:35 Pilate asks Jesus once more, what He has done. How does Jesus respond in verse 36? _____
_____
_____

61. Jesus tells Pilate (and us) clearly in John 18:37 the reason He was born and came into this world. Why was that? _____

62. Jesus defined this truth a couple times earlier in our book of John. Please read John 3:32 and write down what the truth is. _____
_____

63. Now read John 8:47. What does that verse say about the truth Jesus is talking about? _____
_____
_____

64. Flip back to our book of John, Chapter 18 and read verses 38-40.

65. According to verse 38, what basis for charging Jesus did Pilate find?
_____

Go to https://www.gotquestions.org/Azazel-scapegoat.html to read an interesting article about the scape goat concept.

66. John 18: 39-40 introduce us (in an allegorical way) to the Old Testament custom of the scape goat. Please read Leviticus 16:6-10 to learn about this custom. You may also want to spend some time researching the idea of the scape goat using your online bible study tools.

When you are done reading and researching, please summarize what you learned here: _____

_____

_____

_____

_____

_____

_____

_____

67. Thinking back to Jesus' scene in John 18:39-40, how is it an allegorical example of the scapegoat custom we learned about in the question above? _____

_____

_____

_____

_____

68. Use your online study tool to look up the original meaning of the word translated, "atonement" in Leviticus 16:10. What was that word and what did it mean?

_____

_____

_____

It is interesting that this same word is used in Genesis 6:14 when God instructs Noah to build an ark and "cover" it in pitch. Please look that verse up now and consider how God "kaphar-ed" Noah in the ark.

69. In the NIV Study Bible, there is a note on the word translated as "atonement" in Leviticus 16:10 that sends us to Isaiah 53:3-11. Please read those verses now. Who and what are these verses about? _____

_____

Not coincidentally, the day I wrote this portion of our study I received an email from "Chosen People Ministries". Right there, in the middle of a list of prayer requests ranging from praying for President Elect Donald Trump to continue to support Israel, to praying for Holocaust survivors who participated in a beauty pageant, was this:

> "Isaiah53.com Makes a Difference.
>
> Many Israelis are accessing the www.isaiah53.com website in Hebrew and researching and pondering who the Suffering Servant is that Isaiah 53 talks about. This is a great way for Israelis to hear the Gospel in the safety of their own homes. Often in the synagogues, Isaiah 53 is purposefully skipped over so that the clearness of Jesus' death and forgiveness for us is not seen."[9]

70. Now go back to John 18:40 and write down the name of the robber the Jews wanted released instead of Jesus. _____

An in-depth study of the origin of Barabbas' name shows that the original word translated "Barabbas" is G912, Barabbas, and it means "son of a father or master". Looking further into that word, at its origin, we learn that it comes from two words, H1248, bar, which means son, pure and chosen and H5, Abagtha, which means God-given.

71. Using the definitions given to you in the paragraph above, what was the meaning of Barabbas' name? _____

_____

Barabbas; the God-given, pure and chosen son

72. Keeping Barabbas' name in mind as well as all we know and have learned, how is the allegorical scene in John 18:39-40 seemingly confused? Fill in this diagram to help you sort your thoughts:

_____ given to the _____ sacrificed as a _____ offering.

2 goats:

_____ becomes the _____, is freed and used to make atonement for _____.

There is no "one right" answer here. Instead, I am asking you to listen to the Holy Spirit and come up with the answer He is suggesting for you.

When the Jews chose Barabbas over Jesus to be saved, they (unknowingly) did exactly what needed to be done to keep God's perfect plan in motion. God was offering His pure and chosen son, Jesus' life as a sin offering that would make atonement for all mankind's sin so we might be forgiven, pardoned of our sin-debt and free to live an earthly life of peace as well as an everlasting life in relationship with God.

Jesus, not Barabbas (as his name would have you think) was actually God's pure and chosen son who offered His life as a sin offering, making atonement for our sin so we might be forgiven and have an everlasting relationship with God.

No longer would two goats (or any for that matter) be required for a sin offering and atonement. Jesus became both for us on the cross.

73. The Jews' choice of who to free shows just how much they had missed the boat; they saved a robber and killed a king. They were confused over the convicts' true identities. Are you clear about Jesus' identity, who He is and what He's done for you? If so, write about it here: _____

_____

_____

_____

_____

_____

_____

_____

_____

John Chapter Nineteen

CHAPTER 19

1. Spend some time listening to one of your favorite worship songs to get you focused on Jesus. Pray and ask God to teach you through His word as you study it. Ask Him to reveal hidden secrets and to open your eyes to what He wants you to learn in this time.

2. Please read John 19:1-16, envisioning the scene in your mind as it unfolds.

3. Please list the ways the soldiers tormented Jesus according to the first three verses of John 19. _____

_____

_____

_____

4. What does Pilate tell the Jewish crowd in verse 4, regarding his opinion of Jesus' guilt? _____

5. When Jesus came out to the people wearing His crown and robe, Pilate said something. What was that? (see John 19:5) _____

6. Why should we notice John's word choice here? _____

_____

_____

_____

John uses "him/his" (G846) sixteen times in the first sixteen verses of Chapter 19.

7. Another interesting word use in this segment of scripture is the word translated, "him". How many times is a form of the word "him/his" (G846) used in John 19:1-16? _____

8. What purpose do you think John had in using this word so repetitively in these verses? _____

_____

_____

_____

9. What does Pilate say in the second part of John 19:6? _____

_____

"I find no basis for a charge against him."
—Pilate

10. How many times has Pilate said this same phrase? _____

11. In verse 7 the Jews are set on requiring Jesus to "keep the law". What do they say about their law? _____

_____

12. Little did they know that Jesus wouldn't merely keep the law, He would fulfill it. Please read Matthew 5:17, noting Who is speaking, and summarize it here:

_____

_____

_____

"Do not think that I have come to abolish the Law or the Prophets; I have not come to abolish them but to fulfill them."
—Matthew 5:17

13. We see Pilate's indignation for Jesus in John 19:9 and 10. What ironic question does Pilate ask Jesus at the end of this dialogue? _____
   _____

14. Why is Pilate's question so ironic? _____
   _____
   _____
   _____

15. How does Jesus respond to Pilate in John 19:11? _____
   _____

16. Please look up Romans 13:1 and write it here to understand what Jesus meant by His statement to Pilate. _____
   _____
   _____
   _____

"Let everyone be subject to the governing authorities, for there is no authority except that which God has established. The authorities that exist have been established by God."

—Romans 13:1

17. From then on Pilate tried to do something regarding Jesus. What did he try to do according to John 19:12? _____

   Ironically, Jesus already was free and was freely acting on our behalf (and Pilate's), to bring us into relationship with His Father.

18. What does Pilate sit down on in John 19:13? _____

JUST JESUS

19. The original word translated as "judge's seat" in this verse is G968, bema, and it means judgement seat or throne. This same word is used in Romans 14:10 and 2 Corinthians 5:10. What do these verses say?

    - Romans 14:10b – _____

    - 2 Corinthians 5:10 – _____

20. Why is it ironic that Pilate sits down on what he thinks is his judgement seat to judge the Ultimate Judge before whose judgement seat Pilate will one day stand? Discuss. _____
_____
_____
_____

21. How does Pilate introduce Jesus when he presents Him in John 19:14 and how does this introduction differ from the one he gave in John 19:5?
_____
_____

22. Do you think Pilate had a change of heart and now believed Jesus was who He said He was? If not, why do you think he changed the way he introduced Him?
_____
_____
_____

Pilate was perhaps joking when he introduced Jesus as the Jews' "King", but our author, John, wasn't joking at all. He is constantly reminding his readers (us) that Jesus was the Son of God, King of Kings and Lord of Lords. John's use of the word, "King" three times in John 19:14 and 15 demonstrates this.

23. In John 19:15 the priests reject the idea that they are rebelling against Rome but they are in obvious rebellion against Jesus. What does this express about their spiritual condition? _____
_____

24. While Pilate refused to convict Jesus of a crime three times, by the end of our segment of scripture it seems he has lost all resolve to "set Jesus free". How do we know this (see verse 16) and why do you think that is? _____
_____
_____

25. Please read John 19:17-24, picturing the scene in your mind as it unfolds.

26. Who carried Jesus' cross to Golgotha according to verse 17? _____

27. There is a note on the word translated "cross" in John 19:17 in my NIV study bible that leads us to another story where someone carried his own wood for his death. Please read Genesis 22:1-18, noticing the mention of wood in verse 6.

28. The story of Abraham offering Isaac to God is a foreshadowing of God offering Jesus to us and of Jesus offering Himself to us. Please look through Genesis 22:1-8 and write down words you notice are used in Isaac's story that are familiar to you from Jesus' story we've read in the book of John. _____
_____
_____
_____

If you look closely at the story of Isaac, you might also recognize the scapegoat motif we learned about earlier. (see Genesis 22:12 and 13)

JUST JESUS

Look at https://derek-spain.com/2014/03/10/the-answers-30-similarities/ for an interesting article about the similarities between Abraham offering Isaac on Mt. Moriah and God offering Jesus on Mt. Calvary.

29. What does Genesis 22:14 say? _____
_____

Abraham didn't know at that time that God was telling Him that one day, thousands of years later, God would provide the perfect lamb as a sacrifice for all mankind's sins. But God knew.

30. When I read the segment of scripture from Genesis 22:15-18 I cannot read it without hearing it on another level, where God is speaking to His One and Only Son, Jesus. If I paraphrase that conversation it goes something like this,

"The Lord called to Jesus and said because you have done this (My will, offered your life on the cross) and you have not withheld yourself I will bless you and I will make your descendants (followers) as numerous as the stars and the sand. Your followers will conquer their enemies and through them, the fruit of your labor, all nations will be blessed because you have obeyed me."

Can you hear how proud the Father is of His Son? _____

31. Now let's get back to our book of John. Please re-read John 19:17-24.

32. Everything John tells us about the details of Jesus' actual execution is told in one sentence. (see John 19:18) Please write that sentence here: _____
_____
_____
_____

CHAPTER 19

33. Why do you think John told us very few details about Jesus' crucifixion?

_____

_____

_____

34. The picture we get of the three men crucified next to one another is a good example of what Jesus did for mankind on the cross. Three people were crucified and Jesus was in the middle. As our Savior, Jesus is what comes between God and us (He's in the middle) so that we can know God and have relationship with Him. Draw a simple diagram depicting this idea here:

205

JUST JESUS

35. The scene in John 19:19-22 leads us to many questions, but I'm afraid not many answers. Please read these verses and then write down some questions (and possible solutions) you have after reading them. _____

_____

_____

_____

_____

_____

_____

36. What are John 19:23-24 about? _____

_____

"They divide my clothes among them and cast lots for my garment."
—Psalms 22:18

37. The second part of verse 24 tells us why this happened. Please read Psalms 22:18 and write the prophecy here: _____

_____

38. Please read John 19:25-27. How many people were standing near Jesus' cross?

_____

39. In verses 26 and 27 Jesus ensured His mother would be taken care of once He was gone. How did He do this? _____

_____

_____

40. Which disciple did Jesus ask to take care of His mom? (see verse 26)

    _____

41. Did John follow through with Jesus' request to take care of His mother? (see verse 27) _____

42. Please read John 19:28-37. What final "I am" statement does Jesus make in verse 28? _____

43. How does this "I am" statement differ from all of the prior "I am" statements Jesus has made? _____

    _____

    _____

44. What did the soldiers do to satisfy Jesus' thirst? _____

    _____

    _____

This was done to fulfill the prophecy given in Psalms 69:21 that says, "They put gall in my food and gave me vinegar for my thirst." The word translated "hyssop" in John 19:29 is the original word G5301, hyssopos, which was a plant used by the Hebrew people in their ritual sprinklings.

45. Please read Exodus 12:22 and explain how hyssop was used in this segment of scripture. _____

    _____

    _____

> "I am thirsty."
> —Jesus

JUST JESUS

46. Please read Exodus 29:21 and explain the scene here: _____

_____

_____

_____

_____

47. Why, according to the last sentence of Exodus 29:21, did God have the people do this? (see Exodus 29:1 for a hint) _____

_____

48. Please read Leviticus 8:15 and explain the scene: _____

_____

_____

49. What was the purpose of Moses putting blood on the horns of the altar?

_____

50. Why, according to the end of Leviticus 8:15, did Moses consecrate the altar?

_____

51. Please read Leviticus 17:11 and write it here: _____

_____

_____

_____

"For the life of a creature is in the blood, and I have given it to you to make atonement for yourselves on the altar; it is the blood that makes atonement for one's life."

—Leviticus 17:11

52. Now please turn to and read Hebrews 9:19-21. What do these verses say?

    _____

    _____

    _____

    _____

53. What does Hebrews 9:22 say? _____

    _____

    _____

    _____

54. Now let's turn back to the New Testament where we find this same idea in most of the gospels. Please read each of the following verses and write their main points here:

    - Matthew 26:28 – _____

    _____

    - Mark 14:24 – _____

    _____

    - Luke 22:20 – _____

    _____

> "The law requires that nearly everything be cleansed with blood, and without the shedding of blood there is no forgiveness."
>
> —Hebrews 9:22

JUST JESUS

55. Reviewing questions 45–54, please summarize the importance of blood and why Jesus had to shed His blood to save us. _____

_____

_____

_____

_____

_____

56. As you can see, hyssop was used in many important events in scripture. Perhaps one of the most significant times is in Exodus 12:22. What did they use the hyssop for in this verse and why did they do it? _____

_____

_____

_____

_____

"Take a bunch of hyssop, dip it into the blood in the basin and put some of the blood on the top and on both sides of the doorframe."

—Exodus 12:22

57. Why are Jesus being offered vinegar to drink using a hyssop branch and doorframes being sprinkled with blood using a hyssop branch significant?

_____

_____

_____

CHAPTER 19

58. You just finished some deep, serious bible study, friend. Be proud of yourself. I am proud of you. And I bet you've never been more excited to get back to our book of John, so let's go there now. Please turn to John 19:30 and read through verse 37 once more.

59. What does Jesus say in John 19:30 and to what is He referring?

_____

_____

_____

"It is finished."
—John 19:30

60. According to the end of this verse, was Jesus' life taken from Him or did He freely offer it and how do we know? _____

_____

61. Please use your own words to summarize what happens in John 19:31-34.

_____

_____

_____

_____

_____

_____

_____

JUST JESUS

> "The man who saw it has given testimony, and his testimony is true. He knows that he tells the truth, and he testifies so that you also may believe."
>
> —John 19:35

62. Please read John 19:35-37 and summarize it here: _____
_____
_____
_____
_____

63. Please read Numbers 9:12 to learn why it was important that they got Jesus' body down before the Sabbath and why it was important that Jesus not have His legs or any of His bones broken. Why was that? _____
_____
_____
_____

64. Please read the remainder of John 19 (verses 38-42) and explain the scene here:
_____
_____
_____
_____

65. What pieces of information seem most important to you in these verses?
_____
_____
_____

CHAPTER 19

66. Looking back at a few significant verses in John 19, please share your thoughts about them here:

- Verse 28 I am thirsty – _____

    _____

- Verse 29 They gave Jesus a drink of vinegar to satisfy His thirst – _____

    _____

- Verse 30 It is finished – _____

    _____

- Verse 34 A soldier pierced Jesus' side – _____

    _____

    _____

- Verse 38 Joseph asked Pilate for Jesus' body – _____

    _____

    _____

- Verse 39 Nicodemus was with Joseph, preparing Jesus for burial – _____

    _____

    _____

    _____

67. Thinking through all Jesus did for you, as documented in John 19, and why He did it, write Him a prayer of thanksgiving for being willing to go through with His Father's plan: _____

_____

_____

_____

_____

_____

_____

_____

John Chapter Twenty

1. Spend some time listening to one of your favorite worship songs to get you focused on Jesus. Pray and ask God to teach you through His word as you study it. Ask Him to reveal hidden secrets and to open your eyes to what He wants you to learn in this time.

2. Please read John 20:1-31.

3. Now please re-read John 20:1-9 and summarize the scene here: _____
   _____
   _____
   _____
   _____
   _____
   _____

4. What tells us Mary Magdalene felt a sense of urgency once she'd visited the empty tomb? (see verse 2) _____

5. We are told the name of one of the disciples to whom Mary M. ran. What is the other disciple called? _____

6. Who have we come to know that to be? _____

Maybe John refers to himself as the disciple Jesus "loved" because he knew how much Jesus loved him, personally. His faith was based on a personal, intimate relationship with Jesus, and so is ours.

7. It is interesting to note how quickly Mary M. comes up with her own story about what happened to Jesus' body. It doesn't seem like she thought of resurrection for even an instant. What story did she fabricate, according to John 20:2? _____

_____

_____

8. Why was it reasonable for Mary to think this way? _____

_____

_____

_____

9. How often do you jump to conclusions or listen to the stories in your mind instead of remembering what Jesus has told or promised you and how do things usually turn out when you follow that path? What can you do to stay off that path in the future? _____

_____

_____

_____

10. Our author refers to himself as "the other disciple" in verse 3. Why do you think he did that? Do you ever feel like, "the other disciple" and if so, what makes you feel that way? _____

_____

_____

11. What do we learn about our author in John 20:3-9? _____

_____

_____

Our author John was a track star but he was also a scaredy-cat.

12. Please look up John 20:6-7 in the New Living Translation (NLT) to answer this question. What is different about the cloth that had been around Jesus' head than the strips of linen He had been buried in? _____

_____

_____

13. Would a grave robber have likely folded Jesus' head wrap neatly before they stole His body? If not, what does this detail help to prove? _____

_____

_____

Our author makes fun of himself with the word he chooses to start verse 8 with, "finally", because he had finally gotten up the nerve to enter the tomb himself. However, his word choice becomes much more significant when we look at the end of that same verse, where it says, "He saw and believed". Finally, John saw and he believed in all Jesus had taught him, in all Jesus had prophesied about, and in the everlasting life he "finally" had, having chosen to believe.

While I think John's word choice was intentional in verse 8, it's also a bit awkward. We are told he reached the tomb, he went inside and he saw and believed. Please watch the video at cnn.com http://www.cnn.com/videos/tv/2015/02/25/finding-jesus-shroud-3.cnn to see what John may have seen that caused him to instantaneously believe. If the link is not live, feel free to investigate what is known as the Shroud of Turin online on your own.

JUST JESUS

14. Is it possible that John saw Jesus' face on the linens laying in His empty tomb and that is what caused him to "finally" believe? _____

15. John gives us a parenthetical in John 20:9. What is it about? _____

_____

_____

16. In this section of scripture, John shows us an order for sharing the good news. He tells us (or testifies) about Jesus' death and resurrection, and then introduces the idea of Jesus' story being foretold in the scriptures. So, when we are sharing the good news with someone, which should we start with, testimony or the bible?

_____

When introducing others to Christ it is most effective to let others see Jesus' resurrection power in our lives before we lead them to study stories about Him in scripture.

17. Please read John 20:10-18, picturing the scene in your mind as you read.

18. How did the angels address Mary M. in verse 13? _____

19. What did the angels ask Mary M. in this verse? _____

20. How did Mary M. respond? _____

_____

21. What word in Mary's response demonstrates that she had a personal, intimate relationship with Jesus? _____

22. What was Mary M.'s first reaction when she saw Jesus? _____

_____

23. How does Jesus address Mary M. in verse 15? _____

CHAPTER 20

24. Why is it significant that the angels and Jesus addressed Mary M. as "woman"?

_____

_____

_____

> It is significant that we recognize that the first person to see Jesus' empty tomb was a woman and that the first person to whom the resurrected Jesus appeared was a woman. It's important for us to note the respect and sense of equality Jesus had for women as evidenced throughout scripture.

25. What was Jesus' first question for Mary M. in John 20:15? _____

_____

26. This is the second time this same question was asked. If you are a believer, when you look at your life, which of the following questions do you think people ask you more frequently:

- Why are you so downcast and hopeless?

- Why are you so full of hope and joy?

27. Please read 1 Peter 3:15. Keeping it in mind as well as our question options in #26, as followers of Our Resurrected Christ, which question is more fitting for believers' lives and why? _____

_____

_____

_____

28. Why is it important for believers to live lives marked by love and joy rather than being weighted down with worry, fear or hopelessness? _____
_____
_____
_____
_____

29. Mary M. finally recognizes Jesus when He calls her by name in John 20:16. How does this prove that Mary M. followed Jesus? (revisiting John 10:3 and 4 may help you) _____
_____
_____

30. At the end of verse 17 Jesus delineates between God, His Father and God, His followers' Father. How is a follower's relationship with God different than Jesus' was? _____
_____
_____

31. According to verse 18, what did Mary M. do after her encounter with the risen Christ? _____

32. Please read John 20:19-23.

CHAPTER 20

33. How long did the disciples have to wait to see the risen Christ, according to John 20:1 and 19? _____

_____

34. How do we know, according to verse 19, that Jesus used His supernatural power to appear to His disciples? _____

_____

35. What did Jesus say when He stood before His disciples? _____

_____

"Peace be with you!"
—John 20:19

36. Do you think Jesus offered His disciples peace because He saw they were frightened by His appearance or do you think Jesus was reassuring His disciples that He loved them, even after the way they had acted toward Him the week (Passion Week) before? _____

37. Jesus further reassures His disciples in verse 20. What does He do to let them know He's not a ghost? _____

38. In John 20:21 Jesus repeats an idea He prayed in John 17:18. What was that?

_____

_____

39. What did Jesus mean by that and what pattern does it give to us as believers for how we should live our lives? _____

_____

40. Jesus gives His disciples an amazing gift in John 20:22. What was it?

   _____

41. Why do you think Jesus instilled His disciples with the Holy Spirit before the Holy Spirit was sent to all believers, fifty days later at Pentecost? _____

   _____

   _____

John 20:23 is confusing. On the surface it seems like it's saying that God only forgives people if we forgive them, and that God doesn't forgive people if we don't. But that's not at all what Jesus is saying. Instead, He means that when we share the gospel (Jesus' life story) we are offering forgiveness to everyone with whom we share it. Whether or not the person chooses to believe and accept Christ's forgiveness is completely up to them, but the offering of forgiveness has been laid before them.

42. How ought John 20:23 and 2 Peter 3:9 inspire us to share the good news (and therefore forgiveness) with as many people as possible? _____

   _____

   _____

   _____

CHAPTER 20

43. Please read John 20:24-31, then summarize the scene in verses 24-27.

_____

_____

_____

_____

_____

"Unless I see . . . I will not believe."
—John 20:25

44. Thomas was a hard-core skeptic. What three requirements did he have before he would believe? (see verse 25) _____

_____

_____

_____

45. When Thomas sees Jesus a week later in a locked room with the other disciples, what three things does Jesus say to Thomas, after telling him, "Peace be with you."? (see verse 27) _____

_____

_____

_____

46. Would you say that Thomas' requirements were met by Jesus almost exactly and word for word? _____

47. Jesus' last statement to Thomas must have stung a bit. What directive did Jesus give Thomas in John 20:27? _____

"Stop doubting and believe."
—Jesus

JUST JESUS

Our author is reminding us that choosing to enter a relationship with Jesus as our Savior is a personal decision and it's a decision every person has to make for herself. No one else can make that decision for you. It's strictly between you and Jesus.

48. How did Thomas demonstrate that he now acknowledged Jesus as Lord and God? (see verse 28) _____

49. How do we know, from the same verse (28), that Thomas had made a personal decision to follow Jesus as his Lord and God? _____

50. Who do you think Jesus was talking about in John 20:29 when He said, "blessed are those who have not seen and yet have believed"? _____

_____

_____

51. In verse 30 our author tells us that his document isn't an exhaustive account of all the miracles Jesus performed in front of His disciples. What proof do we have (that John didn't have, by the way) that he was right? _____

_____

_____

52. In John 20:31 our author clearly defines his purpose for writing the Book of John. John tells us clearly why he wrote what he wrote about Jesus' life. Why did John write what he wrote according to verse 31? _____

_____

_____

_____

"But these are written that you may believe that Jesus is the Messiah, the Son of God, and that by believing you may have life in his name."

—John 20:31

John Chapter Twenty-One

1. Spend some time listening to one of your favorite worship songs to get you focused on Jesus. Pray and ask God to teach you through His word as you study it. Ask Him to reveal hidden secrets and to open your eyes to what He wants you to learn in this time.

   It seems to me John can't help but throw in one last (HUGE) miracle by Jesus that he had personally witnessed, the Miraculous Catch. He also can't resist showing Jesus as the kind, servant friend He was to His disciples, as He made them breakfast. Perhaps the most important story John wanted to be sure to include in his book was the story about Jesus reinstating Peter, which demonstrated His grace, forgiveness and acceptance of mankind, in its brokenness. All of these are images of a Jesus John knew well and all are examples of how important it was to John for people to understand who Jesus really was, as a person, friend, Savior and Lord.

2. Please read John 21:1-25.

3. Now let's focus in on the last miracle reported in John's book, the Miraculous Catch. Please re-read John 21:1-14 and summarize the scene here:

   _____
   _____
   _____
   _____
   _____

Congratulations on making it to the last chapter in the book of John. Twenty-one chapters - well done! Although this chapter is essentially John's epilogue to his epistle, it's important to note a couple of things before we allow him to close the book on us, pun intended.

4. When the disciples fished on their own, they caught nothing. However, when they did what Jesus told them to do and cast their net on the "right side" of the boat, their catch was miraculous. What underlying message might John have for us regarding the success we will have "fishing for men" on our own, versus "fishing for men" the way or where Jesus tells us to? _____

_____

_____

_____

5. What do you think alerted John to the fact that the man on the shore was Jesus? _____

_____

6. In verse 12 we learn that the disciples, this time, didn't ask Jesus who He was. "They knew it was the Lord". They had come to recognize His voice, His servant heart, and His miracles. How confident are you that you would recognize Jesus if He presented Himself to you today? Do you think you'd ask Him who He was or do you think you'd know it was the Lord? Why do you think that?

_____

_____

_____

_____

How confident are you that you would recognize Jesus if He stood in front of you today?

CHAPTER 21

7. Verse 14 tells us that this fishing and campfire breakfast scene is the third time Jesus appeared to (a group of) His disciples. Why is it important for us to note that?

_____

_____

8. Please read John 21:15-19, picturing the scene in your head as you read it.

9. What does Jesus ask Simon Peter in verse 15? _____

_____

10. Circle which of the following you think is most likely what Jesus was asking with this question:

- Do you love Me more than all this fishing stuff, boat, etc. as He pointed to it?

- Do you love Me more than you love these guys, pointing at the other disciples?

- Do you love Me more than these other guys (disciples) love Me?

11. How many times does Jesus ask Peter if he loves Him? _____

12. How many times does Peter tell Jesus that he loves Him? _____

13. How many times did Peter deny Christ, before the rooster crowed? _____

14. What does Jesus tell Peter to do to demonstrate his love for Him? (see the end of verses 15, 16, 17) _____

_____

According to John 21:15-19, Jesus reminded Peter of His love for him in an effort to reconcile Peter to Himself the same number of times Peter had denied Him, three. Three times Peter denied, and three times Jesus forgave and reinstated Peter as one of His disciples. That's grace.

15. There seems to be a progression in these verses. What does Jesus call His followers in these three verses (John 21:15, 16, and 17)?

Verse 15 _____

Verse 16 _____

Verse 17 _____

In John 21:15-17 Jesus is covering His whole church. He wants His whole body protected and fed; from the baby lambs to the more matured sheep, right up through the sheep who have been in the church long enough to be talking about their deaths. Jesus wants everyone in His church to be nourished by the shepherds He has called into positions of authority within the church, but also by the other sheep. Elder sheep care for middle aged sheep, who in turn, care for the lambs.

16. Where do you fit in this progression of believers? In your discipler role, what are you doing to actively feed sheep who are younger in the faith than you?

_____

_____

_____

17. Jesus prophesies about the kind of death Peter will endure in verse 18. What kind of death was that? _____

CHAPTER 21

18. If you read John 21:18-19 through the lens of Christ's life and death, you can see many parallels. Write the parallels you can pull from these verses. _____

_____

_____

_____

_____

_____

_____

It's as if Jesus is encouraging Peter to have courage and hope through his life journey when He tells him emphatically in verse 19 to "follow Me!".

19. Please read John 21:20-23 and summarize the scene here: _____

_____

_____

_____

_____

_____

20. What was Jesus' point when He responded to Peter in verse 22?

_____

_____

_____

JUST JESUS

> "This is the disciple who testifies to these things and who wrote them down. We know that his testimony is true."
>
> —John 21:24

21. Please read the final two verses in the book of John, John 21:24 and 25. What does our author reveal to us about his identity in verse 24? _____
_____
_____
_____

22. According to John in verse 24, why did he have a "right" to write all these things about Jesus' life? _____

23. Was John's account of Jesus' life all-encompassing or were there some things he left out, according to John 21:25? _____
_____

24. What would have happened to the world if everything Jesus did had been written down? _____
_____

> "Jesus did many other things as well. If every one of them were written down, I suppose that even the whole world would not have room for the books that would be written."
>
> —John 21:25

About This Study

For the Participant
Enter each small group time as well as your personal study time expecting to hear from God. Pray and ask Him to open your eyes and teach you "hidden things". His desire is for us to know Him and one way we get to know Him is by studying His Word. In Jeremiah 29:13, the Lord tells Jeremiah, "You will seek me and find me when you seek me with all your heart." The same is true for us when we are seeking to know Him through His Word. God does not hide from us. He wants to be found and known.

Main Events Page
The page near the beginning of Just Jesus with "Main Events in the book of John" at the top is a tool you can use to make a one-page summary of the main teachings in the book of John. To give you an example, my answer for Chapter 1 was, "Jesus is the Son of God, according to John the Baptist". Fill each chapter blank in as you finish your homework for that chapter and by the time you're done studying the book of John, you'll have a handy-dandy quick reference summary of the entire book.

A Note About Right/Wrong Answers
You may notice there are no answers listed in Just Jesus. While I'd like to say, "there are no wrong answers", I'd be lying. It is possible to study the Word of God and be very far off theologically on your answer. What I'd rather say is, "there are many right answers". Some of the answers may be different for others in your group. They may be different for you at different times, if you do this study more than once. The Holy Spirit is free to teach whoever, whatever, whenever, whyever He wants. Please let Him.

- Be willing to be wrong, but also to be right.
- Be okay with having different answers than anyone or everyone else.
- Allow others to have answers that are different than yours.
- Admit that different doesn't have to mean wrong.

Warning: You will want to know *the* right answer. In fact, you will probably (unconsciously) nominate someone in your group each week to have all the right answers, and that will probably be your small group leader. Please keep in mind that the Holy Spirit wants to teach you, personally, and what He wants to teach you may be different from what He wants to teach others in your small group. It is okay to have different answers. Both answers can be right as long as you remember that both answers can be wrong as well. I suggest you be, as Luke said in Acts 17:11, a Berean who, "received the message with great eagerness and examined the Scriptures every day to see if what Paul said was true." Don't take my answer (or any teacher's answer) as truth. Allow the Holy Spirit to guide you and then test your answers against scripture.

For the Leader

I've included a copy of "Our Small Group Covenant" that I find useful whenever I begin a new season of small group. At our initial meeting, we read through the covenant together out loud and in doing so agree to keep it. Feel free to modify, use or toss it as you feel led.

Another thing I did on day one of Just Jesus that you might consider doing was that I spent time walking my small group through using the online study tool, Blue Letter Bible (www.blueletterbible.org). Online bible study tools can be tremendously helpful, but it's not likely your small group members will use them if they're afraid of them. I tried to take the fear away by taking them through some of the most frequently used and simple tasks. We hooked my laptop up to a tv so they could see what I was doing. Many of my small group told me how much they appreciated the gentle nudge and direction and they felt they actually used the online tools more while doing the study than they would have had I not introduced them to the online study tool.

When studying, "Just Jesus" in a small group, here are a couple things you might consider doing during each of your sessions.

1. **PLAY A WORSHIP SONG ABOUT JESUS**

At the beginning of each session, play a worship song in order to help the group focus their eyes on Jesus and clear their minds of everything else. I have included a song list, but feel free to google "worship songs about Jesus" and use one of your favorites instead. When I thought about including a song list, I wondered if it would be out dated before the study was in print. The point isn't that you use these specific songs, but that you help get your group's mind focused on Jesus.

It is amazing to think that while I may have to worry about a song becoming outdated and ineffective, I never have to worry about the Word of God in that same way. I do not wonder if what God wants to say to you through the book of John will be obsolete someday. Rather, I am confident that if you study John today, what God will teach you through it will most likely be different than what He will teach you if you study it again during a different season of your life. This is true because according to Hebrews 4:12, "the word of God is alive and powerful. It is sharper than the sharpest two-edged sword, cutting between soul and spirit, between joint and marrow." (NLT) The Word is "alive" and "active" or "powerful" and it cuts to the deepest part of us, whoever that is at a specific point in our lives. While God's written word does not change, the effect He has on us through it may.

2. **PRAY FOR YOUR SMALL GROUP TIME**
Allow the Holy Spirit to guide you as you pray for your small group time and for the person who is sharing her testimony that day.

3. **HAVE ONE PERSONAL TESTIMONY SHARED PER SESSION**
"Just Jesus," is John's testimony about his good friend, Jesus. Our personal testimony is just that, "ours". However, we shouldn't be the focus of our testimony; Jesus should be. When asking your group members to write out their "5 minute" personal testimony, remind them why they are doing it; so they will be ready when given the opportunity to share their testimony with people outside of your small group setting.

I have included a "form letter" email you can send the week someone is going to share her testimony in your group. Feel free to copy or modify it as you feel led.

4. **ONCE THE TESTIMONY IS FINISHED HAVE SOMEONE PRAY OVER THE PERSON WHO JUST SHARED HER TESTIMONY AND THEN DIVE INTO YOUR STUDY**

OUR SMALL GROUP COVENANT

The purpose of this covenant is to ensure that the members of this group have shared expectations and values for this small group community. It is our desire to partner with God, through the power of the Holy Spirit, to create an environment where authentic sharing, learning and growing in Christ can take place. We, the members of this small group, make a covenant with one another to contribute to and support the following:

ATTENDANCE AND AVAILABILITY: We agree that we will prioritize regular attendance at our small group sessions, we will arrive on time, and be prepared to participate in discussion and prayer. We will make the group a priority and will make ourselves available to minister to the needs of the others in the group ... helping to meet practical needs when we are able and called by God to do so, as well as supporting one another through prayer (James 2:15-16; Galatians 6:2).

HOMEWORK AND PERSONAL STUDY: We agree that we will prioritize our private bible study time so that we can come each week with a completed lesson, fresh insights we've received from the Lord, and a willingness to share what we've learned with others – that we may be like iron sharpening iron (Proverbs 27:17).

RELATIONSHIPS ARE A PRIORITY: We agree that relationships were a priority to Jesus and while discussion of the curriculum, studying the Scriptures, sharing, and prayer will be the key elements of each session, the driving core value of this group will be the building of relationships ... our individual relationship with the Lord and our relationships with one another (John 13:34-35; Romans 12:10; Galatians 5:13).

AUTHENTICITY AND RESPECT: We agree that this group will be a place where we can be open, honest, and authentic about who we are, questions we have, and ways we may be struggling. We will not however, monopolize our small group sessions with lengthy personal sharing that is more appropriate for a counseling or one-on-one forum (1 Corinthians 13:6; John 8:32; John 16:13)

FINAL AUTHORITY OF SCRIPTURE: We agree that while everyone's thoughts and opinions are valuable and encouraged to be shared, we will ultimately rely on the truth of Scripture as our final authority on all matters of faith (2 Timothy 3:16).

CONFIDENTIALITY: We agree that we will never share with others outside the group any information of a personal nature that was shared during our small group sessions ... this includes prayer request details (Proverbs 11:13; 1 Timothy 3:11)

ABOUT THIS STUDY

RESPECT FOR OTHERS: We agree that we will never share anything that will embarrass or dishonor someone else in the group or outside the group ... this includes inappropriate personal sharing about our spouses, children, church leadership, etc. We agree to keep this small group environment free from gossip, slander and unwholesome talk (Ephesians 4:29).

CONFLICT RESOLUTION: We agree we will seek to reconcile differences, hurts and offenses with each other quickly, directly, prayerfully and lovingly (Galatians 1:6; John 13:35 Colossians 3:13).

GROWTH AND MULTIPLICATION: We agree that healthy small groups grow, and as the Lord directs, we will cheerfully and willingly multiply the group's influence by starting one or more new groups (Philippians 2:3-5).

MEETING TIMES AND SESSION STRUCTURE: We agree to meeting with this small group on (day of the week) from (month – month), with breaks during holiday weeks, from (hour – hour) We understand that our group time will generally consist of opening worship/prayer, sharing of personal testimonies, discussion of the homework curriculum and prayer for one another.

Father, I pray that you will enable me, through my participation in this small group, to be transformed into a more passionate and productive follower of Christ. I commit to do my part and trust you to work in me and through me. In Jesus' Name!

Form letter email for the person sharing his/her testimony

Hi _____,

I want to remind you that you are scheduled to share your life/faith story with our small group this (Thursday). My hope is that GOD WILL BE CENTER STAGE when each person shares her faith story. In other words, I invite you to share the story of your life, your faith journey ... all with a primary mission of giving all the glory to God throughout your time of sharing. Here are some testimony prompts ...

1. Briefly describe your upbringing (family structure, where you grew up and went to high school/college)

2. Briefly describe your current family (husband/children/do you work outside the home)

3. Briefly describe when Jesus entered your life and became your Lord and Savior

4. Briefly describe your spiritual gifts (if you know them) and how are you using them in ministry for the Lord

MAIN FOCUS: *(the majority of your 5 minutes should be spent here)*

5. What is Jesus teaching you in this current season of life?

6. Are you going through any challenges that are helping you to press into God in ways you never have before OR are you in a season of blessing ... tell us about it?

Please pray about what God wants you to share with us and feel free to deviate from this list in any way God leads you to. Please type or write out what you plan to share – not just an outline. Once you've typed or written out your testimony, please time it to be sure you can read it in five minutes or less. We wish we did not have to put a time restriction on testimonies. But, this is good practice at being concise and not sharing more detail than God is leading us to share. This also prepares us to share our story with others outside of small group. We hope you have a rich time of prayer and hear from God what he wants you to share with our group this week.

ABOUT THIS STUDY

Song List for Just Jesus

Always Enough by Casting Crowns
At the Cross by Chris Tomlin
By Our Love by Christy Nockles
Christ is Risen by Matt Maher
Come to Jesus by Chris Rice
Forever by Kari Jobe
Glorious Day by Casting Crowns
Go Tell it on the Mountain by any Christian artist
Healer by Kari Jobe
Help Me Believe by Nichole Nordeman
Here Is Love by Bethel Live
Holy and Anointed One by Mercy Me
I Can Only Imagine by Mercy Me
I Know You're There by Casting Crowns
In Christ Alone by Phillips, Craig and Dean
Jesus Hold Me Now by Casting Crowns
Jesus Lead Me to Your Healing Waters by David Crowder Band
Jesus Loves Me by Whitney Houston or anyone
Jesus Paid It All by Passion (feat. Kristian Stanfill)
Jesus, Son of God by Brandon Heath
Just Give Me Jesus by Jeremy Camp
King of my Heart by Love and the Outcome
Lead Me to the Cross by Francesca Battistelli

Like Jesus Does by Eric Church
Love Came Down by Bethel Live
Mercy by Casting Crowns
My Master by Christy Nockles
Never Once by Matt Redman
No Not One by Christy Nockles
Our God by Chris Tomlin
Personal Jesus by Johnny Cash
Power to Redeem by Lauren Daigle
Show Jesus by Jamie Grace
The Day Love was Born by Dara Maclean
There is Something About that Name by Bill Gaither
This I Believe by Hillsong Worship
To Know You by Casting Crowns
To Know You by Nichole Nordeman
Trust in Jesus by Third Day
Untitled Hymn by Chris Rice
Walk on Water by Britt Nicole
Welcome to Our World by Chris Tomlin
What a Beautiful Name by Hillsong Worship
What a Friend We Have in Jesus by Aretha Franklin or Alan Jackson
Wonderful Name by Christy Nockels

Works Cited

Chapter 4

1. redemption. Dictionary.com. Collins English Dictionary - Complete & Unabridged 10th Edition. HarperCollins Publishers. http://www.dictionary.com/browse/redemption (accessed: April 27, 2018).

2. Kohn, Rabbi Daniel. "What Are Pilgrimage Festivals?" *My Jewish Learning*, 70/FACES Media, 27 Apr. 2018, www.myjewishlearning.com/article/pilgrimage-festivals/.

Chapter 6

3. Grossbaum, Rabbi Yossi. "Spiritual Anorexia." Spiritual Anorexia, 26 Aug. 2016. rabbi@jewishfolsom.org

Chapter 10

4. Henry, Matthew. "Commentary on John 10." Blue Letter Bible. 1 Mar, 1996. Web. 4 Oct, 2016. <https://www.blueletterbible.org//Comm/mhc/Jhn/Jhn_010.cfm>.

Chapter 11

5. Henry, Matthew. "Commentary on John 11." Blue Letter Bible. 1 Mar, 1996. Web. 4 Oct, 2016. <https://www.blueletterbible.org//Comm/mhc/Jhn/Jhn_011.cfm>.

6. Guzik, David. "Study Guide for John 11." Blue Letter Bible. 7 Jul, 2006. Web. 5 Oct, 2016. <https://www.blueletterbible.org/Comm/guzik_david/StudyGuide_Jhn/Jhn_11.cfm>.

Chapter 12

7. Stek, John H. "Baker's Evangelical Dictionary of Biblical Theology." Edited by Walter A. Ellwell, Biblestudytools.com, Baker Books, www.biblestudytools.com/dictionaries/bakers-evangelical-dictionary/hosanna.html.

Chapter 17

8. unity. Dictionary.com. Dictionary.com Unabridged. Random House, Inc. http://www.dictionary.com/browse/unity (accessed: April 27, 2018)

WORKS CITED

Chapter 18

9. "Inside Israel; Isaiah53.com Makes a Difference." Chosen People Ministries, Nov. 2016, chosenpeople.com/site/inside-israel-november/.

Additional resources used:

www.blueletterbible.org
All definitions of original Greek/Hebrew words were taken from www.blueletterbible.org

Strong's Concordance

The Bible Knowledge Commentary

Life Application Study Bible, NIV

Life Application Study Bible, NLT

Bible, KJV

The Message

www.ingramcontent.com/pod-product-compliance
Lightning Source LLC
Chambersburg PA
CBHW060419010526
44118CB00017B/2284